# BOUND FOR THE NORTH STAR

# BOUND FOR THE NORTH STAR

## True Stories of Fugitive Slaves

DENNIS BRINDELL FRADIN

CLARION BOOKS ★ NEW YORK

Clarion Books
a Houghton Mifflin Company imprint
215 Park Avenue South, New York, NY 10003

Copyright © 2000 by Dennis Brindell Fradin
Picture research: Judith Bloom Fradin

The type for this book was set in 12-point Bodoni Book.

www.hmco.com/trade

Printed in the U.S.A.

*Library of Congress Cataloging-in-Publication Data*
Fradin, Dennis B.
Bound for the North Star : true stories of fugitive slaves / by Dennis Brindell Fradin.
p.   cm.
Includes bibliographical references and index.
ISBN 0-395-97017-2
1. Fugitive slaves—United States—Biography—Juvenile literature.
2. Underground railroad—Juvenile literature.
3. Abolitionists—United States—Juvenile literature.
4. Antislavery movements—United States—Juvenile literature.
I. Title.

E450.F77 2000
973.7'115—dc21    00-029052

EB  10  9  8  7  6  5  4  3  2  1

*For Lauren Michelle Bloom and David Philip Bloom,*
*with love from Uncle Dennis*

# ACKNOWLEDGMENTS

*For their gracious assistance, the author thanks:*
*Fran Filko and Robin Jindra, Oberlin Senior Center;*
*Whitney Pape, Oberlin College Library Special Collections;*
*Roland Baumann and Tammy Martin, Oberlin College Archives*

# CONTENTS

A NOTE FROM THE AUTHOR     xi

1    MARY PRINCE     1
*"Oh, the Horrors of Slavery!"*

2    FED     12
*"Bound for the North Star"*

3    ELIZA HARRIS AND MARGARET GARNER     32
*My Child Shall Not Be a Slave*

4    PETER AND VINA STILL     44
*"I Am a Slave No More!"*

5    HENRY "BOX" BROWN AND LEAR GREEN     66
*"Go and Get a Box and Put Yourself in It"*

6    ELLEN AND WILLIAM CRAFT     80
*"A Desperate Leap for Liberty"*

7    WILLIAM WELLS BROWN     97
*"Now Try to Get Your Liberty!"*

8    THE OBERLIN-WELLINGTON RESCUE OF JOHN PRICE     111
*"They Can't Have Him!"*

9    JOHN ANDERSON     130
*"No Man Should Take Me Alive!"*

10    ANN MARIA WEEMS     147
*"My Child, Is It Really You?"*

11    SOLOMON NORTHUP     155
*Nobody Knew His Name*

12    HARRIET TUBMAN     182
*"My People Are Free!"*

AFTERWORD     196
*Slavery Is Still with Us*

BIBLIOGRAPHY     199

INDEX     202

*White trader inspecting an African before carrying him to America as a slave*

# A NOTE FROM THE AUTHOR

Slavery is the next thing to hell," Harriet Tubman said in 1856. "If a person would send another into bondage, he would be bad enough to send him into hell if he could."

The Indians were the first people in the New World to be enslaved. Christopher Columbus began capturing and enslaving them during his famous exploration of 1492–93. As European colonists came to North, South, and Central America, and to the islands of the West Indies, they forced the Indians to mine treasure and grow their crops. At times, Indian slaves rebelled or escaped, but millions of them died of overwork and cruel treatment; the result was the destruction of entire tribes.

When the supply of Native Americans ran low, European colonists turned to Africa for slaves. Nearly fifteen million Africans were kidnapped and sent to various places in the New World between the 1500s and the 1800s. Slavery began in England's American colonies in 1619 with the arrival of about twenty black people in Jamestown, Virginia. The slave population of the thirteen colonies had reached 500,000 by 1776. On July 4 of that year, the American colonists adopted the Declaration of Independence, announcing that

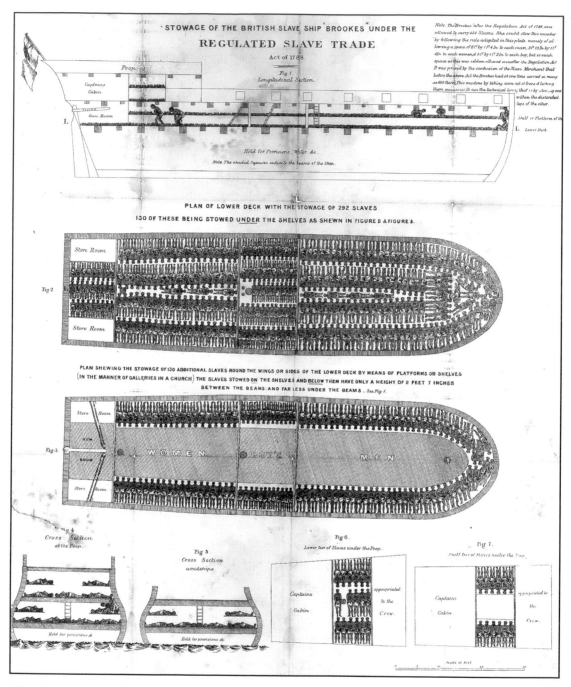

*On the voyage to America, slaves were packed into ships, as this plan of the British vessel* Brookes *shows.*

the thirteen colonies had become the United States. Although the Declaration asserted that "all men are created equal" and are entitled to "Life, Liberty, and the pursuit of Happiness," all thirteen of the new states permitted slavery and excluded slaves from these basic freedoms.

In 1780, Massachusetts became the first state to outlaw slavery. Other northern states followed, until slavery was ended in the North by the mid-1800s. Southern planters kept adding to their slave holdings, however, especially after the invention of the cotton gin in 1793 made cotton a huge moneymaking crop. By 1850, there were 3.2 million slaves in the South—one seventh of the nation's population. Many of the slaves grew "King Cotton," but some were house slaves, while others with special skills such as carpentry or haircutting worked in town, earning large sums of money for their owners.

*Slaves on a ship; they are near starvation.*

Slave life was so harsh it is difficult to imagine. Picture working in a cotton, tobacco, or rice field sixteen hours a day; being whipped by an overseer if you fall behind in your work; living with your family in a tiny cabin with a dirt floor; eating only moldy corn and bacon; wearing your only set of clothes day after day; possessing nothing of your own, often not even a last name; having no more rights than a horse or a cow, so that your master can kill you or rape your mother and sisters if he wants; watching helplessly as your relatives are sold to different owners, never to see one another again; being forbidden to learn to read and write; having to show a pass to every white person

*Slaves were brought into Virginia in the 1600s.*

you meet when away from home; and worshiping in the "Negro section" of the church, where the white preacher says you will go to hell, should you defy your master or run away. Finally, imagine that if you are caught trying to escape, you may be branded with a red-hot iron, whipped nearly to death, or burned at the stake. If you can imagine all that, you may begin to have some idea of what slavery was like.

When abolitionists argued that slavery was wrong and must be ended, southern whites often argued that slaves didn't have such a bad life. The slaves thought otherwise. After Tennessee passed a law in 1858 allowing free black people to voluntarily return to slavery, not one person accepted the offer. And if slavery wasn't so bad, why, despite the tremendous risks, did fifty thousand slaves flee to the North and to Canada, while hundreds of thousands of others were captured trying to escape?

The story of the slaves who fled in quest of liberty is one of the most exciting chapters in all of history. Making their way through forests and swamps, the fugitives usually traveled at night, guided by the North Star. Often they were helped along by the Underground Railroad, a network of hiding places established by abolitionists, where runaways could eat and rest on their trip northward.

To this day, many American families speak with pride of ancestors who fled slavery or who hid runaway slaves in their homes. Few of these stories have been written down, however. Not having been taught to read and write, the fugitives were generally unable to record their experiences. Also, because anything written about fugitive slaves might be used in court to have them returned to bondage, Underground Railroad "conductors" generally kept sketchy notes, at best.

Fortunately, a small number of fugitive slave narratives were put in writing. After going to school, several escaped slaves wrote about

*Newspaper advertisement for a slave sale in South Carolina in the late 1700s*

their experiences, often using pseudonyms to make it more difficult for their former owners to locate them. Then in 1865 the North defeated the South in the Civil War, ending slavery forever in the United States. With no fear of being returned to bondage, more ex-slaves chronicled their escapes. In addition, a few Underground Railroad workers, notably William Still and Levi Coffin, kept detailed notes about the escaped slaves they had helped and later wrote books about them.

Books about such fugitive slaves as Harriet Tubman, Henry "Box" Brown, and Ellen and William Craft were popular among nineteenth-century readers. Then, as now, they provided inspiring examples of how human beings, in their desire for liberty, can overcome incredible difficulties. But the stories of the escaped slaves did more than that. They awakened thousands of readers to the evils of slavery, helping to bring on the struggle that freed more than four million people who hadn't been fortunate enough to escape.

*A slave auction in Richmond, Virginia*

# CHAPTER ONE

# MARY PRINCE

## *"Oh, the Horrors of Slavery!"*

*After the thirteen colonies declared their independence and became the United States of America in 1776, Great Britain still ruled many other lands in the New World, including Canada and the islands of Bermuda, Jamaica, and the Bahamas. Like the newborn United States, the British territories allowed slavery. A slave woman named Mary Prince helped convince British lawmakers to outlaw slavery thirty-two years before the United States did so.*

Mary Prince was born around 1788 on a farm in Bermuda, an island 640 miles east of North Carolina. Mary's mother was a house slave and her father was owned by a shipbuilder. When Mary was an infant, a sea captain purchased her and her mother. At first, Mary was a playmate of the captain's granddaughter, Betsey, who was her age. "I was made quite a pet of by Miss Betsey, and loved her very much," Mary recalled, many years later. "She used to lead me about by the hand, and call me her 'little nigger.' This was the happiest period of my life, for I was too young to understand my condition as a slave, and too thoughtless and full of spirits to look forward to the days of toil and sorrow."

Mary's parents were allowed to spend Saturday night and Sunday together. Three more girls and two boys were born to them after Mary. Since Mary's mother belonged to the sea captain, all of her children were automatically his property, too.

When Mary was twelve years old, the sea captain's family needed money and decided to sell Mary and two of her sisters. On the day of the sale, Mary knew something bad was happening, for her mother couldn't stop crying. She dressed Mary and her sisters Hannah and Dinah in their best clothes, saying bitterly, "See, I am shrouding my poor children. What a task for a mother!" Mary never forgot those words, but only when much older did she understand that "shrouding" means "dressing for burial."

Mary's mother finished dressing her three daughters and then told Miss Betsey, "Take your last look at them. Maybe you will see them no more. I must take my little chickens to market."

Their mother took the three girls to the market in Hamilton (now Bermuda's capital), where she was under orders to sell them at the slave auction.

Strange men came up to Mary and her sisters, feeling their muscles and examining their teeth to determine the girls' worth. As the oldest, Mary was sold first. The bidding began at a few pounds and gradually increased. When it ended she had been bought by a man for fifty-seven pounds in Bermudan currency, equal to nearly $200 in U.S. money. Spectators tried to console Mary by saying that she had brought her master a lot of money for so young a girl, but by this time she understood that she had been sold, and she was sobbing. Within a few minutes, her sisters had also been sold. "When the sale was over, my mother hugged and kissed us, and mourned over us," Mary Prince later recalled. "It was a sad parting. One went one way, one

*Often parents and children were separated if sold to different owners.*

another, and our poor mother went home with nothing." Their mother
said farewell to her daughters by telling them to "keep up a good
heart," meaning a brave spirit.

Mary's new owners, Captain and Mrs. I. (she never did reveal
more than the first letter of their last name) took her to their home in
another part of Bermuda. The terrified girl entered their house and
stood in a corner crying, "Oh, my mother! My mother! My mother and
my sisters and my brothers, shall I never see you again?"

"You are not come here to stand up in corners and cry," Mrs. I.
said gruffly. "You are come here to work!" She placed her baby in
Mary's arms, ordering her to take care of the child.

The next morning, Mrs. I. told Mary that besides serving as the
baby's nursemaid she was to wash floors, pick cotton, and cook. When
her work didn't satisfy them, Captain and Mrs. I. punched Mary with
their fists or whipped her. Once when she broke a jar, Captain I. tied
her up and gave her a hundred lashes as his young son stood by and
kept count. The only kindness Mary received was from Hetty, a slave

in the household who was pregnant. One day a cow that Hetty was watching broke loose. Captain I. whipped Hetty so savagely that she lost her baby and became very ill. Shortly afterward, she died.

Mary was then given all of Hetty's tasks in addition to her own. She was doing the morning milking when a cow got loose and ate some sweet potatoes in the garden. Captain I. punished Mary by taking off his heavy boot and slamming it against her back. As Mary shrieked in pain, the frightened cow kicked over the milk pail, angering Captain I. even more. He whipped the badly injured girl until she fell to the ground, nearly unconscious.

Slaves who ran away were sometimes killed as an example to others, but Mary felt that she had nothing to lose. She ran away to her mother, who hid her in a cavern along the seacoast, bringing her food at night. Her mother didn't know what to do, for the longer Mary was gone, the more severe her punishment was likely to be. Finally, she asked Mary's father, who was called Prince, to take her back and speak to Captain I.

Mary's father was in a very difficult position. He wanted to convince her owners to forgive Mary, yet, as a slave himself, he had to be careful what he said to a white man. "Sir," he told Captain I., "I am sorry that my child should be forced to run away, but the treatment she has received is enough to break her heart. The sight of her wounds has nearly broken mine. I entreat you, for the love of God, to forgive her for running away, and that you will be a kind master to her in future."

Her owners did not whip her for running away, but they soon resumed the "same harsh treatment" of her, as Mary later reported. She remained with Captain and Mrs. I. for five years in all, until she was seventeen. Then she was sold to a Mr. D., who lived in the Turks Islands, a British territory east of Cuba. Mary begged to say good-bye to her parents, brothers, and sisters, but her request was refused. Provisions ran low during the four-week, eight-hundred-mile voyage to the Turks Islands. If not for a couple who shared their food with her, Mary might have starved.

Mary had hoped that her life would be better with her new master, but it was far worse. Mr. D. had bought her to work in his salt pond with his other slaves. Fifteen hours a day, she stood up to her knees in the water with her barrel and shovel, mining salt from the pond. "The Sun flamed upon our heads like fire," she remembered in later years, and "our feet and legs, from standing in the salt water for so many hours, soon became full of dreadful boils, which ate in some cases to our very bones, afflicting the sufferers with great torment." But Mr. D. expected his slaves to shovel a certain amount of salt each day, no matter how they felt. If slaves didn't work fast enough, he hanged them by the wrists and whipped them until blood poured down their backs. He would then throw a bucket of salt on their wounds to increase their pain.

"Oh, the horrors of slavery—how the thought of it pains my heart!" Mary Prince later said about her five years working in the salt ponds in the Turks Islands.

Mr. D.'s son, Master Dickey, served as his overseer. Master Dickey's ambition seemed to be to surpass his father in cruelty. Once while a slave named Ben was being hanged from the ceiling by his wrists because hunger had driven him to take a little rice without permission, Master Dickey stabbed him through the foot with a bayonet. Another time, when an elderly slave named Sarah didn't push her wheelbarrow fast enough to suit him, Master Dickey picked her up and threw her into a patch of prickly pear cactus. The cuts from the prickles became infected, and Sarah died a few days later.

Around 1810, Mr. D. retired to Bermuda, taking Mary along. She was happy to return to her birthplace. Her father had died while she was in the Turks Islands, but she was occasionally allowed to visit her mother, sisters, and brothers. Mary was assigned to do the household work, grow bananas and other crops, and wait upon Mr. D.'s daughters, but she soon learned that Mr. D. had additional plans for her. He raped her whenever he wanted. As his property, Mary could not stop Mr. D. from forcing her to have sex with him, for he might kill her if she resisted.

Mary Prince remained Mr. D.'s slave on Bermuda for six years. Since escape from the little island was nearly impossible, her only recourse was to beg Mr. D. to sell her to a new owner. Around 1816, he sold her for one hundred pounds in Bermudan currency, or approximately $300, to a couple named Wood, who wanted to take her with them as their house slave to the island of Antigua. Mary made the thousand-mile voyage with high hopes, for Antigua offered more opportunities for slaves to buy their own freedom than the other British-ruled islands.

Mary did the housekeeping for Mr. and Mrs. Wood and cared for their baby. She began to think about earning her freedom, for if her owners would allow her to work for others on Sunday (the slaves' day off), in a few years she might earn enough money to buy herself out of slavery. Soon after her arrival on Antigua, however, Mary became very ill.

She suffered from severe arthritis, made worse by years of beatings and hard work. Although only twenty-eight years old, she had to walk with a cane because her left leg was crippled. Despite her condition, her new owners made her go down to the pond to wash clothes and continue with her other tasks. A skin infection spread across her

## CASH!

All persons that have SLAVES to dispose of, will do well by giving me a call, as I will give the

### HIGHEST PRICE FOR

# Men, Women, & CHILDREN.

Any person that wishes to sell, will call at Hill's tavern, or at Shannon Hill for me, and any information they want will be promptly attended to.

**Thomas Griggs.**

Charlestown, May 7, 1835.

PRINTED AT THE FREE PRESS OFFICE, CHARLESTOWN.

*Slave dealers bought slaves and then sold them at a profit. This advertisement was issued by a South Carolina slave dealer.*

crippled leg, and soon she couldn't even stand. Repulsed by Mary's skin condition, Mr. and Mrs. Wood threw her out of their house and sent her out to a shed in their yard—either to recover or to die. For weeks she lay in the darkness on the floor, too weak to push the insects off her infected leg, her only food a daily meal shoved under the door. Fortunately, a neighbor heard her groans and sent over an old slave woman and a doctor to care for her, or she probably would have died.

Mary recovered after several months and was allowed back in the house. As her strength returned, she became more determined than ever to buy herself out of slavery. Now and then, her owners went on trips, leaving Mary to look after their home. On these occasions, Mary earned a little money by taking in washing and selling yams that she grew in her garden.

In 1826, when she was in her late thirties, Mary met a carpenter named Daniel James. Daniel became the love of her life and a great inspiration, for he had purchased his own freedom with money he had earned while a slave. At Christmastime, Mary and Daniel were married.

When they learned of the marriage, Mr. and Mrs. Wood were enraged. "I will not have a nigger man in my house, or allow a nigger man's clothes to be washed in the same tub as mine!" Mrs. Wood exclaimed. Mr. Wood beat Mary with his horsewhip for failing to ask permission to be married. "It's very hard to be whipped at my age just for getting a husband!" Mary bitterly protested. They relented somewhat, allowing Daniel to live in the shed in their yard.

At this time, Mary asked her owners how much she would have to pay to buy her freedom. She had saved the equivalent of about $100 during her ten years with them and she was so worn out and ill with arthritis that she figured she wasn't worth much more than that. But at the word "freedom," they became very angry. "Who put the idea of freedom into your head, you black devil?" Mrs. Wood demanded.

It was her own idea, Mary answered. "To be free is very sweet," she said, but her master and mistress refused to consider her plea.

In 1828, Mr. and Mrs. Wood sailed to England to enroll their son in school, taking Mary along. She said good-bye to Daniel, expecting to return to Antigua in a few months and resume her attempts at freedom.

Mr. and Mrs. Wood thought they could accomplish in England what they had failed to do in Antigua—crush Mary's proud spirit and cure her of her desire for freedom. They had told her that they were taking her to England to care for their son, but once in London they also ordered her to cook and clean, although her arthritis was again making it difficult for her to walk. When Mary complained, they mocked her and told her she was free to go if she didn't like how she was being treated.

"I will never sell you your freedom in Antigua," said Mr. Wood. "If you wish to be free, you are free here in England. Go try what freedom will do for you, and be damned!" he taunted her, opening the door.

Mary wanted to leave the Woods, but she was afraid, for where would a sick, friendless, aging slave woman find refuge in the world's largest city? Twice over the next few weeks Mr. and Mrs. Wood made the same mocking offer. Again, she was tempted to go, but as they laughed and said she was sure to become a beggar or be murdered, she was overwhelmed by fear of the unknown.

After several months in London, Mary had an argument with her master and mistress over the washing. For the fourth time, they opened the door and said she could leave. This time she astonished them—and perhaps herself, too. Barely able to walk, she hobbled out the door without saying a word and left them staring after her in amazement.

Out on the London streets, someone directed Mary to the mission house of the Moravian Church, a religious group that would help her. She was offered refuge at the Moravian mission house. Only once did she return to the Woods- –to fetch her belongings.

By 1828, when Mary Prince seized the opportunity to be free, the British people were engaged in a tremendous debate: Some wanted to end slavery in the British Empire, while others wanted it to continue. Among the abolitionists who met with Mary were Thomas Pringle, secretary of the Anti-Slavery Society in London, and his wife, Margaret. The Pringles welcomed her into their home, where Margaret Pringle taught her to read and write.

One day Thomas Pringle asked Mary if she wanted to return to Antigua. "I wish to go back to my husband very much, very much, *very* much," she answered, "but I am much afraid my owners would separate me from my husband, and sell me." Mary also told Pringle

*A painting showing the freeing of the slaves in the 1830s
in the British islands of the West Indies*

that she wanted to leave a record of her life story. "I want it to be done
that people can hear from a slave what a slave has felt and suffered,"
she explained. And so she related her life story to a friend of the
Pringles, who wrote it down. The book was published in England and
Scotland in 1831 under the title *The History of Mary Prince, A West
Indian Slave, Related by Herself.* The first autobiography as well as
the first antislavery work published by a British black woman, the
book was an immediate success.

Among its readers were many members of Parliament, Great Britain's lawmaking body. The book helped convince Parliament to pass an act in August 1833, which was to take effect August 1, 1834, ending slavery throughout the British Empire. In Antigua, the Bahamas, Bermuda, Jamaica, England, Canada—wherever the British flag flew—the slaves were freed and slavery was outlawed.

By the time her book was published, Mary Prince was going blind. What became of her is unknown, for she disappeared from history in 1833, when she was about forty-five years old. After the slaves were freed in Antigua in 1834, did she return to the island to be with her husband? Did Daniel leave Antigua and join her in England? The answers to these questions are not known, but it is certain that, through the power of the written word, Mary Prince helped liberate many thousands of slaves throughout the British Empire.

# CHAPTER TWO

# FED

## *"Bound for the North Star"*

*S*laves generally did not know their birthdate, for they weren't taught to read or shown calendars. And not only did they have no permanent last name, many slaves didn't even have a first name of their own. Instead, they were called by several first names, according to their owners' whims. For example, a slave boy who was born in Virginia around 1810 was sometimes known as Benford because his father belonged to a man by that name, but he was usually called Fed, for reasons he never was able to learn.

Fed, his three brothers and two sisters, and their mother, Nancy, belonged to a wealthy widow named Betty Moore. At one time Fed's father, Joe, had lived on a nearby plantation, but he had been sent far away during Fed's early childhood. Only once in Fed's memory was his father allowed to visit the family. During their brief time together, Joe told Fed that their ancestors had been members of the Ibo people, from the part of Africa that is now Nigeria. Many years earlier, Fed's grandfather had been stolen from his home and taken across the ocean to America by slave traders.

The seven members of Fed's immediate family lived with several cousins, making a total of about twelve people in their two-room cabin. At about the age of four, Fed was given his first job, caring for his baby brother while their mother worked all day in the tobacco fields.

Each morning Betty Moore put the slave children through a routine that she said would make them "grow likely for market." First she made them line up outside her big plantation house and open their mouths while she poured a foul concoction made of garlic down their throats. Then, so that they would learn to move quickly, the children had to race around a large sycamore tree in the yard. Mrs. Moore kept a whip dangling from her belt, and she used it on any child who didn't run fast enough to please her. Since the whip was painted blue, the children called it the blue lizard.

*Benford or Fed,*
*later known as John Brown*

Fed was nine when talk of a "great trouble" spread through Mrs. Moore's plantation. At night, Fed's mother would sneak out to the field to whisper with the other adults and then return to the cabin crying. On a bright autumn morning around tobacco harvest time, the slaves were ordered to gather in the yard, where Mrs. Moore and several of her relatives were seated on chairs beneath the sycamore tree. Mrs. Moore, who was about seventy years old, was keeping some of her slaves but distributing the rest to her family. The slaves were divided into four lots, or groups. Fed's brother Silas and sister Lucy, who were twins, were to remain with Mrs. Moore. Fed and the rest of his family were to go to North Carolina with Mrs. Moore's son-in-law, James Davis, who was said to be an extremely cruel man.

That night there were many tearful farewells on Mrs. Moore's plantation. Early the next morning, the slaves were herded into carts. As his cart pulled away, Fed looked upon his brother Silas and his sister Lucy for the last time.

Mr. Davis lived up to his dreadful reputation. The only food he provided his slaves was corn, and he whipped them for slight infractions. Ten-year-old Fed worked sixteen hours a day alongside his mother, growing cotton and tobacco. One hot day Fed and his little brother picked and ate a watermelon from Davis's garden. Unfortunately, Mr. Davis was watching. He grabbed Fed and whipped him until the boy could scarcely move. Weeks passed before Fed recovered.

Among their tasks, the slave children were expected to pick worms off the tobacco plants and rip them to pieces. Davis inspected the tobacco leaves himself. He made the children eat any worms that they had overlooked. "That will teach you to have sharper eyes in the future!" he said.

*A slave being weighed and sold by the pound*

Fed remained at Davis's for a year and a half. Then Davis offered him for sale to a slave dealer, who agreed to pay four dollars a pound for him. Fed was hoisted up onto a big scale. After his weight was calculated, the slave dealer handed Davis $310.

The dealer marched Fed off to join his other slaves, who were handcuffed and chained in a double row beyond the Davis gate. Seeing her son being led away, Fed's mother rushed toward him and begged to be permitted to kiss him good-bye, but the slave dealer slammed the gate in her face. The last Fed saw of his mother, she was standing by the gate weeping.

The next few weeks were a blur to Fed, who had been separated from his entire family. With the other slaves, he was marched five hundred miles through North and South Carolina into central Georgia. There he was sold to Thomas Stevens, who grew cotton and corn on his plantation near Milledgeville, which was then Georgia's capital. Stevens sometimes found the twelve-year-old boy standing in the field staring into space because he felt so downhearted. Stevens would beat Fed, but no matter how hard the blows, the boy didn't seem to care.

One day Stevens accused Fed of running too slowly when he

*Slaves preparing cotton for the cotton gin on a South Carolina plantation*

sent him on an errand a mile away. He decided to give Fed a beating that would take the blank expression off his face. "Why didn't you run, sir?" demanded Stevens, pulling out his knife and cutting a hickory rod.

"I *did* run, sir," Fed answered.

"Oh, you ran, did you?" Stevens said, and beat him so furiously that the hickory rod was destroyed.

"Now, sir, you tell me you ran?" Stevens repeated.

"Yes, sir," insisted Fed, refusing to give in despite the blood running down his back.

Stevens cut another hickory rod and again beat Fed. "Why don't you cry, sir, why don't you cry?" demanded Stevens, his rage growing as Fed neither shed tears nor admitted wrongdoing. He beat Fed with a third, fourth, and fifth hickory rod. Fed was barely conscious and covered with blood when an elderly slave ran up to Stevens and begged, "Oh, master, please don't kill the poor boy. He hasn't got the sense to cry!" But Stevens went on beating Fed, stopping only because a visitor arrived while he was cutting a sixth hickory rod.

As the years passed, Fed became close friends with John Glasgow, a slave whose life had been as tragic as his own. Born free in Guyana, a South American country then claimed by Great Britain, John had gone to sea in his youth. He had settled in England, married a white woman, and lived with her and their two children on a farm near Liverpool. To help support his family, John Glasgow had decided to go to sea again. Around 1830, he had sailed to America with an English captain to pick up a cargo of rice in Savannah, Georgia. Upon his arrival, John was kidnapped from the ship and sold to Thomas Stevens, who beat him for insisting that he was a free black man with a wife and children in England. Most of the 300,000 free black people in the United States at that time lived in the North, for in the South free blacks were routinely seized and sold into slavery.

John Glasgow became almost like a father to Fed. He told Fed that, for his own sake, he must try not to think about his mother and other relatives. He also advised Fed to try to escape across the ocean to England, which in 1834 would prohibit slavery. Fed listened to John Glasgow's stories about England and dreamed of one day fleeing there.

Thomas Stevens hated Fed and John Glasgow for what he called their "brave looks and nigger pride," and he often tried to "flog their nigger pride out of them." One day while Fed was plowing the cotton field, Stevens came up and asked why he was doing a poor job. As Fed stooped down to show him that the plow was broken, Stevens suddenly kicked him in the head, breaking his nose and turning his right eye around in its socket.

Despite his terrible injuries, Fed had to finish his day's work. Later, in the slave quarters, John Glasgow washed the blood from Fed's face, pushed his eye back into place, and bound it with a handkerchief. Fed could barely see out of his right eye for the rest of his life, but the blow helped him in one way. He vowed that he would escape slavery or die trying.

His first attempt came a short time later. A notorious outlaw named John Murrell operated a gang of "Negro stealers," who lured slaves away by promising to take them north to freedom. But instead of freeing them, Murrell's gang sold the slaves to new masters, at a huge profit for themselves. Around the age of twenty, Fed ran off with Buck Hurd, a member of Murrell's gang. They hadn't gone far when

Hurd learned that Murrell had been captured and sentenced to prison. Fearing that he, too, would be caught, Hurd pulled out a gun and forced Fed to return to the Stevens plantation. Hurd told Thomas Stevens that he had captured Fed running away and received a reward of $30 for bringing him back. Fed was fortunate. In other cases when they suspected that their scheme might be uncovered, Murrell's gang shot slaves.

Fed expected a severe punishment for running away, but he wasn't even whipped, perhaps because Thomas Stevens was ill. Soon after, Stevens suffered a stroke that paralyzed him and eventually took his life. Fed was inherited by Thomas's son, Decatur Stevens, a dim-witted man who lived in the vicinity of present-day Atlanta, Georgia. His new master grew to rely upon Fed, who was skilled at farming and carpentry and so strong that he could "do the work of two slaves," as Decatur Stevens bragged to his friends. Decatur even seemed to fear Fed. Occasionally, Fed would hide for a few days in the woods—a temporary escape known as lying-out, which many slaves engaged in from time to time. Upon Fed's return, Decatur Stevens would not whip him but would hide behind bushes and throw rocks at him. He didn't realize it, but Fed was awaiting the opportunity to run away permanently.

Once while lying-out in the woods, Fed met a poor white man. In exchange for an old hen that Fed had stolen from Decatur Stevens, the white man forged a pass for him. A few weeks later, Fed walked out of his cabin at night with his pass in his pocket.

Thinking that England was just a short way off, he walked all night. At daybreak he hid in the woods and swamps, searching for berries and other plant foods. He resumed his journey after sundown. Farther and farther northward Fed walked, until he was stopped by mountains in

Tennessee. He was trying to find a way around this barrier when he encountered a white man chopping wood.

"Where's your pass, sir?" demanded the man.

Fed handed the pass to the man, who studied it briefly and said it was obviously fake. However, he promised that if Fed accompanied him to his home he would help him escape. Once there, the white man sent for five armed friends, who helped him lock Fed in chains and question him about his owner. Anticipating a reward for capturing his runaway slave, the men dispatched a messenger to Decatur Stevens.

While his captors awaited word from Stevens, Fed was taken to the home of one of the men, where he was chained to the wall. After nearly a week of imprisonment, Fed managed to break the chain. In a moment, he was out the door and running. Not knowing where else to go, he retraced his steps and in several days was back at the plantation of Decatur Stevens, who this time gave him a dreadful beating.

After that, Fed appeared to change his ways. He acted humble around Stevens, pretending to be afraid of him. To test whether Fed would now obey him, Stevens sent him into a barn to catch two slave boys whom he intended to whip. But when Fed didn't try his best to catch the boys, Stevens ordered an old slave woman to fetch his gun. Realizing that Stevens intended to shoot him or the boys—or all three of them—Fed knocked his master to the ground and dashed out of the barn into the woods.

For three days, Fed hid in an apple orchard while Stevens rounded up friends and a dog pack to hunt him down. One of the men found Fed and smashed him in the head with a wooden club. Fed awoke to find his head bleeding and Decatur Stevens standing

*Pursuit of a fugitive slave*

with his foot on his forehead. Stevens and his friends took turns whipping Fed until he passed out. Then Stevens attached a metal torture device called bells and horns to his head. Once this twelve-pound helmet was locked in place, Fed could barely stand, let alone run; and if he did attempt to escape, Stevens would be warned by the bells. "Run off now if you like!" dared Stevens as Fed regained consciousness.

Fed had to wear the bells and horns day and night. The weight

*Woman wearing bells and horns
to prevent her from running away*

was a constant torment to his head and neck, especially when he bent
down, for he still had to work in the fields. Night offered no relief, for
he was unable to lie flat, and he could only sleep for an hour or two
at a time, crouching. His friend John Glasgow had been given away
to Decatur Stevens's brother, but during the three months that Fed
wore the bells and horns, he found comfort in recalling John's stories
about his life in England as a free man.

One day, Decatur Stevens ordered Fed to pack corn into the corn-
crib. Fed insisted that he couldn't do it with the bells and horns on
his head. Certain that Fed no longer had the strength or will to flee,
Stevens removed the device. As soon as Stevens was out of sight, Fed
ran away.

Fed believed that if he went in the general direction he had traveled earlier—but this time bypassed the mountains—he would reach a river that led to England. With no knowledge of geography, he had no idea that England was more than four thousand miles away across a broad ocean.

Night after night he walked beneath the stars, sometimes covering thirty miles before sunrise. He slept by day in the hollows of trees or in rock shelters, and survived by digging up sweet potatoes and cooking them in fires that he started with dry sticks.

In Alabama, he came to a river that he hoped might take him to England. He built a raft and floated along this waterway (the Tennessee River) into Tennessee and then Kentucky. Fed had been traveling along the river for many nights when suddenly a fearsome monster, hissing and belching smoke, approached him. Never having seen a steamboat before, he thought it was the Devil. Fed paddled his raft as fast as he could to the shore, abandoned it, and ran toward some lights. He had arrived at Paducah, Kentucky, located where the Tennessee and Ohio Rivers meet.

Fed had traveled five hundred miles to reach Paducah. Now all he had to do to be free was cross the Ohio River into Illinois. Although he could actually *see* Illinois from Paducah, he didn't realize that he was looking at free soil. Besides, he was terrified that at any moment someone would capture him and return him to Decatur Stevens.

Seeing more steamboats around Paducah, Fed figured out what they were. He found a vessel bound for New Orleans, which he believed might be near England, and persuaded the captain to let him travel on the steamer. Fed claimed that he had been separated from his master and needed to meet him in New Orleans.

The steamboat headed down the Ohio River to the Mississippi

River, then followed the great river south. For nearly a thousand miles Fed journeyed downriver, unaware that with each mile he was traveling farther from freedom. The morning he arrived in New Orleans, Fed stepped off the vessel and found a group of slaves unloading cotton along the waterfront. Questioning them, Fed learned that New Orleans was deep in slave territory and that he was farther from England than he had been in Georgia.

Fed walked through the closely patrolled streets of New Orleans, expecting to be arrested as a runaway slave at any moment. He formed a desperate plan. He would get himself sold to a better master than Decatur Stevens, find out where England was, and await another opportunity to run away.

Fed studied the faces of people walking by and picked out a young white man as a likely prospect. Judging by his gold-headed cane, rumpled clothing, and bloodshot eyes, Fed figured the man had spent the night drinking and gambling and needed money. Fed approached him and said, "I've run away, sir, from the state of Georgia. I thought you might take me and sell me, and put the money in your pocket, so that my old master may never get me anymore."

The young man told Fed to wait while he entered a nearby slave auction house. He returned with Theophilus Freeman, a prominent New Orleans slave dealer. Freeman looked Fed over and asked to see the papers proving that the young man owned him. He had inherited Fed from his father, the young man lied, and had no bill of sale. Freeman said that without a bill of sale he would pay $400 for Fed instead of the $800 the young man sought. As he pocketed the $400 for selling a slave he didn't own, the young man walked away cursing Freeman for cheating him. Freeman then led Fed to the "Negro pen," as the auction house was called.

Five hundred slaves were crowded into the three-story building. Fed was surprised that Freeman and his partners fed and clothed the slaves well, and dyed the hair of those who had turned gray. He soon realized that this was to make the slaves "likely for market," as Betty Moore used to say. Each day, customers came to buy slaves. The auctioneers took pride in their ability to pass off a sick, old slave as young and healthy, so any slave who failed to "look bright and smart" in front of customers was chained to the floor of the flogging room in the attic and beaten with paddles. Whips weren't used because they would "damage the merchandise" by cutting the skin.

While Fed was in the Negro pen, a slave named George was brought in, locked in irons. He was chained up because he had been caught running away. George informed Fed that his best chance of gaining his freedom was by fleeing to the northern states up the Mississippi, which could be recognized by its muddy waters.

Fed decided to try to get bought by someone who lived near the Mississippi River. By the time Fed had been in the auction house for three months, Theophilus Freeman began to suspect that he wasn't doing his best to look bright and smart. Fed was threatened with the flogging room if he wasn't purchased soon. A few days later, buyers from up the Mississippi River arrived. A planter named Jepsey James approached Fed, felt his muscles, and examined his injured eye. Although he later said that James struck him as a "sour-looking" man, Fed did his best to appear eager and obedient. Jepsey James paid $1,200 for Fed, and took him by steamboat to his home on the "shirt-tail bend" of the river near Greenville, Mississippi.

The James plantation was in the Mississippi Delta, land so fertile that people claimed silver dollars sprouted on the cotton plants. Fed was put to work picking cotton from four in the morning until nightfall. On his first day, he picked more than the one hundred pounds expected of him. Seeing that Fed was a good worker, James demanded that he do even better. He ordered him whipped until he reached the mark of 160 pounds of cotton a day. Something else about Jepsey James disturbed Fed: Although most slave owners spared pregnant women the lash, James whipped them as severely as he did his other slaves, causing some of them to lose their unborn children.

From where he worked in the fields, Fed could see the Mississippi River about five hundred feet away. He noticed that a small rowboat was kept near the shore. One night when he had been on the James plantation for several months, Fed crept from his cabin,

*A stereoscopic photograph of slaves picking cotton*

dragged the boat down to the river, and rowed about a mile to the Arkansas side. He then turned the boat adrift, letting the river's current carry it southward. If Jepsey James found the boat, he might guess that Fed was returning to New Orleans. Actually, he was walking the opposite way, toward the north.

He walked by night and hid by day, as he had done on his earlier attempts. While wading through swampy areas along the river, he had to avoid alligators splashing about in the darkness. Often he found nothing to eat but sassafras buds and pine roots. For about three months he continued on, more exhausted each day.

After he had walked six hundred miles, he reached a large city. Fed decided to take a chance and speak to a black man he saw on a steamboat along the shore. He boarded the vessel and was given some bread and beef by the man, who was the cook. The man informed Fed that he was in St. Louis in the slave state of Missouri, just across the river from Illinois.

He was still talking to the cook when the captain of the steamer noticed Fed and approached as if to grab him. Fed quickly slipped off the opposite side of the vessel. He found a small boat tied to a tree alongshore and rowed across the river to Illinois. He had learned enough geography from George in New Orleans to know that Illinois was a free state—something he hadn't understood on that earlier escape attempt when he had come so close to freedom. He also knew that, to be truly safe, he must travel much farther north. The United States had a fugitive slave law, dating from 1793, allowing owners to recover runaway slaves from free states. But the farther north fugitives went, the less easily their former owners could pursue them.

Over the next few weeks, Fed walked through the free states of

# $100 REWARD!

## RANAWAY

**From the undersigned, living on Current River, about twelve miles above Doniphan,** in Ripley County, Mo., on 2nd of March, 1860, **A NE GRO MAN,** about 30 years old, weighs about 160 pounds; high forehead, with a scar on it; had on brown pants and coat very much worn, and an old black wool hat; shoes size No. 11.

The above reward will be given to any person who may apprehend this said negro ou. of the State ; and fifty dollars if apprehended in this State outside of Ripley county, or $25 if taken in Ripley county.

**APOS TUCKER.**

*Poster offering reward for runaway slave from Missouri*

Illinois and Indiana. He met many people who offered him shelter. On the road to Vandalia, Illinois, he stayed with a black man who advised him to change his name to make it more difficult for his former master to find him. Fed chose the name John Brown—perhaps in honor of his friend John Glasgow.

Near Indianapolis, Indiana, a black man who was painting a fence seemed to recognize John Brown (Fed) and advised him that he was in grave danger. Jepsey James had posted advertisements around the countryside offering a large reward for his capture. The posters described Fed's injured eye and scars, making it easy for him to be identified. At that very moment, professional slave hunters were combing the countryside, hoping to capture him and claim the reward.

The fence painter directed John Brown to a settlement of Quakers, a religious group that strongly opposed slavery. Once there, he was welcomed at a house by two young men, who introduced him to their father as "another of the travelers bound for the North Star," a secret way of saying he was a fugitive slave heading north. When the father clasped John Brown's hand and introduced him to his wife, John nearly cried. Never before had he been treated so kindly by white people.

His hosts fed him the best meal of his life and showed him to a comfortable bed. Years later, John Brown recalled how he felt when he awoke during the night:

> *In the middle of the night I awoke, and finding myself in a strange place, became alarmed. It was a clear, starlight night. . . . I felt so happy, notwithstanding my fear at not being able to make out where I was, that I could only conclude I was in a dream, or a vision, and for some minutes I could not rid my mind of this idea. At last I became alive to the truth, that I was in a friend's house, and that I really was free and safe. I had never learnt to pray; but if what passed in my heart that night was not prayer, I am sure I shall never pray as long as I live. I cannot describe the blessed happiness I enjoyed.*

John remained with this Quaker family for eight days. But as word of his presence spread, the father of the family told him, "Friend John, it is not safe for thee to stay any longer." Accompanied by the family's two sons, John rode on horseback to another home that was part of the Underground Railroad. On his trip through Indiana, John may have stayed with the couple Levi and Katie Coffin, who helped so many runaway slaves that Levi was nicknamed the President of the Underground Railroad.

From Indiana, John Brown continued north to Marshall, Michigan, where he lived with a group of escaped slaves for a year and helped them build a church. From there he went to Detroit, Michigan, where he met a group of miners from England.

At this time, around 1848, a "copper rush" was occurring in Michigan's Upper Peninsula, along Lake Superior. The English miners asked John to accompany them to the Upper Peninsula to work as a miners' carpenter. A remote region with vast forests and few people, the Upper Peninsula was one of the safest places in the United States for escaped slaves. John and the miners traveled by boat up through the Great Lakes to Copper Harbor, at the Upper Peninsula's northern tip. John Brown had now traveled nearly two thousand miles from Mississippi, mostly on foot, to reach safety in northern Michigan's Copper Range.

For eighteen months he worked as a miners' carpenter. To be paid for his work and to be treated like a man—*to be free*—was a new and wonderful experience for John Brown. When his miner friends returned to England, John went on to Canada, where he worked at a sawmill for about six months. He helped saw the wood used in the Canadian exhibit at the first world's fair, the Great Exhibition of 1851 held in London, England. He also invented a device that transported timber through the water to the sawmill.

John Brown still cherished an old dream. The last he had heard, John Glasgow had suffered a shattered leg after being struck by a falling oak tree that he had chopped down. Glasgow would never be able to escape to his wife and children. But John remembered Glasgow's advice—that if he ever had the chance he should go to England. In the summer of 1850 Brown sailed to England, where he lived the rest of his life.

John learned to read and write in his adopted country. In 1855, with the help of an abolitionist there, he published *Slave Life in Georgia*, the story of his experiences and journey to freedom. Whether he ever married or located John Glasgow's family remains unknown. John Brown, formerly known as Benford and Fed, lived quietly in England for twenty-six years, working as a carpenter. He died in London in 1876, at the age of sixty-six.

# CHAPTER THREE

# ELIZA HARRIS AND MARGARET GARNER

## My Child Shall Not Be a Slave

*Although most slaves who escaped were men, some of the most heroic attempts were made by women. Upon learning that their children were about to be taken from them, mothers were known to carry their sons and daughters hundreds of miles to freedom. Eliza Harris and Margaret Garner were two slave mothers who fled with their children— with very different outcomes.*

Eliza lived in Kentucky, a few miles south of the Ohio River, which separated her home state from the free soil of Ohio. She had three children, but as often happened among the poorly fed, ill-treated slave families, two of them died very young. Eliza was left with one child, who became the center of her life.

One winter day, Eliza learned that her owners were about to sell some of their slaves and that she and her two-year-old child were to be separated. She didn't hesitate. She took the baby in her arms and walked all night, reaching the Ohio River at dawn.

During some winters the river froze solid, enabling escaped

slaves to dash across the ice to freedom on the Ohio bank. But as the sun rose, Eliza saw that the quarter-mile-wide river was only partially frozen. Large chunks of ice floated by, sometimes breaking apart and plunging into the water. Realizing that crossing the river was virtually impossible, and afraid that her child would freeze to death if they stayed outside much longer, Eliza knocked on the door of a house near the riverbank. Fortunately, the inhabitants sympathized with the fugitives and invited them inside to eat and rest.

Eliza planned to wait until the middle of the night to search for a way to cross the river. But in the early evening, slave hunters sent by her owners tracked her to the house where she had taken refuge. As the slave hunters closed in on horseback, Eliza clutched the baby to her chest and ran out the back door of the house, determined to reach the opposite shore or die in the attempt.

Her pursuers chased her to the riverbank and were about to seize her when Eliza leaped onto a floating piece of ice with her child. The men watched in amazement as the slave mother and child floated down the river a short way on the miniature iceberg. Just when the floating ice began to break apart and it seemed that the fugitives would drown, Eliza jumped, holding her child, to another cake of drifting ice.

Slowly Eliza crossed the river with her precious bundle, leaping from one floating piece of ice to another. Sometimes she had to toss her child onto the next floe and then jump into the freezing water and pull herself up. Her hands, arms, and legs were almost frozen, but she drove herself on toward the Ohio shore.

Eliza's heroic struggle ended when she and her child reached the bank near the town of Ripley, Ohio. She was so exhausted and bruised from the ordeal that she fell to the ground. A man who had

*Eliza crossing the ice with her child,
as portrayed in* Uncle Tom's Cabin

been watching from the Ohio side, and who had expected them to sink beneath the raging water at any moment, helped them up the riverbank. When Eliza was able to walk, the man led her and the child to the house of Reverend John Rankin, a prominent Underground Railroad worker in Ripley.

Reverend Rankin provided the mother and child with food and dry clothing. Eliza and her baby spent only about an hour or two with him, however, for the slave hunters might still be in pursuit. The fugitives were sent across the state line to the home of Levi and Katie Coffin in Newport (today Fountain City), Indiana.

Levi and Katie were among the most active members of the Underground Railroad, sheltering more than two thousand fugitive slaves during their twenty years in Newport. Some people claimed that the Coffins inspired the name "Underground Railroad," or "UGRR," as the network was known for short. Supposedly it was coined when slave hunters from Kentucky chased a group of fugitives to the vicinity of the Coffins' house. As they did so often, Levi and Katie hid the fugitives in secret rooms before sending them farther north during the night. One of the frustrated slave hunters commented, "There must be an underground railroad [meaning a train that ran beneath the ground], and Levi Coffin must be its president, and his house the Grand Central Station."

UGRR workers began using railroad terminology to disguise their activities. Abolitionists who arranged for slaves to flee northward became known as "ticket agents." People like the Coffins and Reverend John Rankin who hid slaves were called "stationmasters," and their homes were referred to as "stations" or "depots." Those who, like Harriet Tubman, led slaves northward were known as "conductors," while those who assisted the "passengers" once they reached free soil, such as William Still of Philadelphia, were "brakemen." Successful escapes were "smooth trips," and when trouble occurred it was said that "the train was run off the track." This secret language was useful, for if a letter fell into the wrong hands or a conversation was overheard, the UGRR workers could claim they were referring to trains, not slave escapes.

Forwarded from station to station by UGRR conductors, Eliza and her baby had a smooth trip to Levi and Katie Coffin's house in

*Levi Coffin*

*Katie Coffin*

Newport. The Coffins gave them refuge for several days. Besides caring for Eliza and her child, Katie Coffin gave them a last name of their own: Harris. Eliza Harris became so attached to the couple that she began to call Mrs. Coffin "Aunt Katie."

After a few days, Levi Coffin sent Eliza and her child northward, perhaps hiding them in a wagon with a false bottom. Taking refuge in a series of UGRR stations, generally about fifteen miles apart, they finally reached Sandusky, Ohio. From there they crossed Lake Erie to Canada. They settled in Chatham, Canada, where a colony of escaped slaves from the United States lived.

In the summer of 1851, Levi and Katie Coffin took a trip to Canada with an abolitionist friend, Laura Haviland of Michigan. They were at a meeting at a church in Chatham when a woman suddenly approached Mrs. Coffin and said, "How are you, Aunt Katie? God bless you!" It was Eliza Harris. Eliza invited the Coffins and Laura Haviland to her home in Chatham, where they found the mother and child "comfortable and contented," as Levi Coffin wrote in his book, *Reminiscences of Levi Coffin,* which was published when he was seventy-eight years old, long after slavery had ended.

In 1851–52, the American writer Harriet Beecher Stowe published her famous novel *Uncle Tom's Cabin.* Many people, including Abraham Lincoln, credited this antislavery novel with helping to bring on the Civil War, which ended slavery in the United States. In one moving scene, a fleeing slave named Eliza, holding her child, crosses the ice-choked Ohio River. This scene was based on the real-life heroism of Eliza Harris, the slave mother who escaped to Canada with the help of Levi and Katie Coffin.

⸺⸱⸺

After twenty years in Newport, Indiana, Levi and Katie Coffin moved to Cincinnati, Ohio, in 1847. Lying just north of Kentucky across the

*Levi and Katie Coffin's home in Newport, Indiana, was a UGRR station.*

Ohio River, Cincinnati was a busy UGRR stop. Levi and Katie sheltered 1,100 fugitive slaves while in Cincinnati, raising the total number of escaped slaves they aided to more than 3,100. One of the great sorrows of their lives was that they weren't able to help a fugitive slave named Margaret Garner and her family.

In the winter of 1855–56, the Ohio River froze solid. Fearing that their slaves would flee across the ice to the free soil of Ohio, Kentucky slaveholders became very watchful. In January 1856, however, a slave family from far northern Kentucky formed a daring plan. They would take a sleigh and two horses belonging to one of their masters and race over the snow to the river. Those involved in this escape attempt included a woman in her twenties named Margaret Garner, Margaret's husband, Robert, the couple's four children, and Robert's parents.

The family got into the sleigh late on a Sunday night and sped across the snow toward the Ohio River. Near dawn they reached Covington, Kentucky, where they abandoned the horses and sleigh and crossed the frozen river on foot to the Cincinnati side.

Margaret Garner and her family were seen by a number of people as they made their way along the Cincinnati waterfront to the home of the Kite family, free blacks who were relatives of Margaret's. The Kites were worried that the fugitives would be tracked to their house. After the runaways ate breakfast, Margaret's cousin Elijah Kite went to talk to Levi Coffin at his store at the corner of Sixth and Elm Streets. The President of the UGRR said that the fugitives were in grave danger at the Kites' house. Coffin directed Elijah Kite to take them to a mostly black neighborhood in Cincinnati where escaped slaves were often sheltered. As Kite hurried home to move the Garners to this safer area, Levi Coffin made plans to send them northward that night along the UGRR.

A few years earlier, Margaret Garner and her family might have

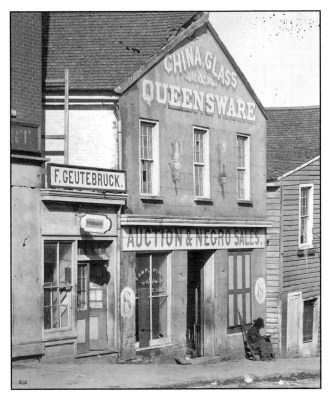

*A slave auction house in Atlanta, Georgia*

been safe at the Kites' house. Although the 1793 Fugitive Slave Law had allowed slaveholders to pursue runaways to the North, few had done so because of the trouble and expense. With the argument over slavery intensifying, the U.S. government appeased white southerners in 1850 by enacting a new law that made it easier for slave owners to capture runaways. Signed into effect on September 18 by President Millard Fillmore, the Fugitive Slave Law of 1850 made it a federal offense to "harbor or conceal" a runaway slave; people who helped a slave escape could be ordered to pay a $2,000 fine and serve six months in jail. Furthermore, law officers were expected to help slaveholders locate and arrest runaway slaves, and "all citizens," regardless of their views on slavery, were "commanded to assist" in identifying and seizing fugitive slaves.

To abolitionists like Levi and Katie Coffin, the Fugitive Slave Law was a national disgrace. Obeying what they called a Higher Law—the law of right and wrong—they continued to help runaway slaves, despite the personal risks. But because most people were afraid to break the new federal law, there was no longer any place on U.S. soil where escaped slaves were safe. Growing numbers of fugitives headed all the way north to Canada, where slavery was illegal and where their owners couldn't pursue them. Runaways were reluc-

*A slave auction*

tant to spend even a single night in border cities like Cincinnati, where they could be arrested with relative ease.

Elijah Kite arrived home from Levi Coffin's store too late. Minutes after his return, the owners of Margaret Garner and her family, together with law officers and a posse of proslavery men, surrounded his house. The Garners decided to fight and die rather than be captured. Margaret Garner declared to her mother-in-law, "Mother, before my children shall be taken back to Kentucky, I will kill every one of them!" Margaret's husband was armed, and when a deputy marshal broke a window and tried to enter the house, Robert Garner shot and wounded him. But the slave hunters battered down the door, rushed inside, and overpowered Robert.

With the family's dream of freedom shattered, Margaret Garner grabbed a knife that was lying on a table and cut the throat of her two-and-a-half-year-old daughter, Mary, killing her instantly. She was attempting to kill her three other children and herself when she was seized by the slave catchers and taken to jail.

The Margaret Garner case stunned the nation. Americans wondered: How could a mother kill her own child, whom she claimed to love? Abolitionists called the killing an act of love and kindness, for slavery was so oppressive that death was preferable. They pointed out that Margaret Garner had acted in keeping with Patrick Henry's declaration from Revolutionary times: "Give me liberty or give me death!" On the other hand, proslavery people claimed that she was simply a deranged killer.

In a bizarre turn of events, Margaret Garner became the object of a legal tug-of-war between Ohio and Kentucky. Ohioans wanted her tried for murder, so that the world could learn about the horrors of slavery. Kentuckians wanted her returned according to the Fugitive

*Margaret Garner killed two of her children rather than return them to slavery.*

Slave Law, so that her owners could determine what to do with her. The federal government held a trial in Cincinnati to decide what to do with Margaret Garner. Levi Coffin attended the trial and later reported on it in his *Reminiscences*. He wrote that Garner was about five feet tall and had scars covering her head. When asked what had caused the scars, she responded, "White man struck me." Coffin added:

> *During the trial she would look up occasionally, for an instant, with a timid, apprehensive glance at the strange faces around her, but her eyes were generally cast down, and her general expression was one of extreme sadness. The case seemed to stir every heart that was alive to the emotions of humanity. The interest was not so much for the*

*legal principles involved, as for the instincts that mold every human heart—the undying love of freedom that is planted in every breast—the resolve to die rather than submit to a life of degradation and bondage.*

The federal court ruled that Margaret Garner and her family should be returned to their owners, who could decide their fate. Margaret was taken to a Kentucky jail, where she was held for a few days. Soon after, she and her family were sold to another planter. While being transported by boat to her new owner, Margaret jumped into the water with her year-old daughter, Priscilla, in her arms. The baby drowned, but Margaret Garner was pulled from the water against her will by the boat's crew and sent on to her new master. Margaret and Robert Garner and their two remaining children, Thomas and Samuel, eventually were sent to a Mississippi cotton plantation. Margaret made no further attempts on the lives of her two sons. In 1858 she died of typhoid fever, at the age of only twenty-five. Her last words to Robert were "Live in hope of freedom."

Levi Coffin included the story of Margaret Garner in his *Reminiscences* to remind us that many slave escapes ended in disaster. About a hundred years after his book was published, the African American writer Toni Morrison learned about the Margaret Garner story. It inspired her to write her novel *Beloved*, which won the 1988 Pulitzer Prize.

# CHAPTER FOUR

# PETER AND VINA STILL
## *"I Am a Slave No More!"*

*To escape slavery, patience was often as important as courage. Many years could pass before an opportunity to flee arose. Peter Griffin— later known as Peter Still—had to wait half a century for his chance at freedom.*

Peter was born on the Eastern Shore of Maryland around the year 1800. Soon after Peter's birth, his father informed the family's owner, Saunders Griffin, that he would kill himself if he remained a slave. Rather than lose a valuable piece of property, Mr. Griffin offered him the chance to purchase his freedom. In addition to his regular work, Peter's father did odd jobs on Sundays and late at night for dimes and quarters. In about 1804, he bought himself out of slavery. Before going north, he told his wife to flee with their four children at the first opportunity and join him at a secret place in New Jersey.

A year or so later, Peter's mother ran off with him, his older brother, Levin, and their two little sisters, Mahalah and Kitturah. They made their way to New Jersey, where they located Peter's father. The family's reunion was brief, however. Slave hunters tracked down the mother and four children and dragged them back to Saunders

Griffin. To prevent Peter's mother from attempting another escape, Mr. Griffin locked her in the attic of his mansion at the end of each workday and kept her there all night.

After several months, Master Griffin concluded that the slave woman had been cured of her desire to run away and permitted her to rejoin her four children in their cabin. But Peter's mother was more determined than ever to escape. Since fleeing with all four children seemed impossible, she reluctantly decided to leave her two sons behind and escape with the girls. Later, she hoped, she and her husband would find a way to rescue Peter and Levin. On a summer night in about 1806, she kissed her sleeping sons good-bye, then headed north with her daughters.

Peter and Levin awoke in the morning to find their mother and

*Peter Still*

sisters gone and their master in a rage. Saunders Griffin decided to sell eight-year-old Levin and six-year-old Peter so that their parents would never find them. But before the boys were led away, their grandmother, who also lived on the Griffin plantation, told them a secret: Their parents and sisters had settled along the Delaware River somewhere near Philadelphia, Pennsylvania.

The parents and two daughters had actually settled on the New Jersey side of the river, in a remote woodland called the Pine Barrens. They adopted Still as their last name and changed their first names, too, so that slave hunters would have trouble identifying them. Over the years, the couple had thirteen more children, at least six of whom lived to adulthood. The Stills earned a living by chopping wood and growing vegetables. In time, their son James grew up to be a doctor, their daughter Mary became a teacher, and their youngest child, William Still, became a famous abolitionist. But the parents suffered from an enormous grief, for they had left behind two sons in Maryland who had been sold to someone in an unknown location. As their other children were growing up, the Stills often spoke to them about their "two lost brothers" who remained in slavery.

Peter and Levin had been taken to Lexington, Kentucky, where they became the slaves of a brickmaker. At first, the boys cried for their mother and begged the brickmaker to return them to her. Their master would "become a monster," Peter later recalled, kicking and whipping them until they acknowledged that they were his property. Thereafter, only when they were alone did the boys talk about their family and discuss the possibility that their mother or father would rescue them.

For a while, the brothers did chores around their master's plantation. At the age of nine, Levin was put to work in the brickyard, and

*Charity Still,*
*Peter and Levin's mother*

*William Still*

Peter soon followed. At an age when today's children are in elementary school, the brothers worked all day making bricks.

In 1813, their master sold thirteen-year-old Peter and fifteen-year-old Levin for $450 apiece to another Lexington brickmaker, Nat Gist, who was known for his drunken rages. Not long after he bought the brothers, "Master Nattie" came home drunk and ordered Peter to feed his horse. Peter did as he was told, but Gist angrily demanded, "Why the devil did you throw the oats all about?"

"Why, master," answered Peter, "*you* told me to scatter them."

Gist whipped Peter brutally for talking sassy. "I mean to make a good nigger of you," he said, "and there's no way to do it, only by showing you who's master!"

After Levin and Peter had worked in his brickyard for about three years, Mr. Gist hired them out to work in a Lexington tobacco factory for a year. The factory owner paid Gist rent for the brothers. By now Peter and Levin realized that their parents did not know where they were. At night in their cabin, they whispered about running away or buying themselves out of slavery. But Lexington was closely patrolled for runaways, and they knew of many slaves who had tried to buy their liberty, only to be cheated out of both their money and their freedom. A man they knew named Spencer had saved for many years to purchase himself. His master took the money, but instead of gaining his liberty, Spencer was sent to the cotton fields of the Deep South. Unless they were sold to someone they trusted, the brothers agreed, they would not try to buy their freedom.

Peter barely survived the year at the tobacco factory. One day, Mr. Norton, the factory owner, inflicted three hundred lashes on a slave, then slammed a board with nails embedded in it into the man's back, gouging out huge pieces of flesh. The other slaves at the tobacco factory who witnessed this brutal deed were paralyzed with fear, but Peter said to his brother, "I will die before I allow him to do that to me!" Someone overheard Peter's words and repeated them to Mr. Norton.

Later, while Levin was away on an errand, Mr. Norton decided to punish Peter for his remark. "Lie down across this box!" he ordered, preparing to beat him with a stick. To the factory owner's amazement, Peter replied, "I have done nothing wrong. I will not lie down!"

Mr. Norton called for several white men to help him grab Peter. They approached Peter with a noose, threatening to hang him.

Fighting desperately, he escaped the noose, but the white men finally overpowered him. Mr. Norton whipped him for more than an hour, all the while cursing him for being "the first nigger that ever tried to fight me." Norton and his friends then went off to eat breakfast, leaving Peter to crawl out of the factory and back to the home of Nat Gist, his owner. Mr. Gist granted Peter a week to recover. Then he returned him to the tobacco factory with a warning that Mr. Norton must not damage his property again.

*Plantation slave cabins in South Carolina*

The next year, 1817, three of Nat Gist's nephews moved south, near Tuscumbia, Alabama. To help one of the nephews establish a farm and store, Mr. Gist gave him Levin and five other slaves as a going-away present. Peter and Levin begged Mr. Gist not to separate them, but it was in vain. "I shan't ever see you again!" Peter cried, as his brother began the three-hundred-mile trip to Alabama.

A year later, Nat Gist died, and Levin's owner in Alabama inherited Peter. On a cold December morning, Peter was led away on horseback. Seventeen days later, he arrived at a plantation along the Tennessee River in northern Alabama, where Levin was waiting for him.

The brothers worked for the Gist nephews for more than ten years. They picked cotton, swept their store, and served as house slaves. When Levin reached the age of twenty-four, he asked permission to marry a young woman named Fanny from a nearby plantation. Levi Gist, the nephew who owned Levin and Peter, said no. Children born to slaves were the property of the mother's owner, which meant that if Levin married Fanny, their children would belong to Fanny's master. Levin must marry a woman from his own plantation, Levi Gist ordered, so that their children would be *his* property. But Levin and Fanny loved each other and married without Levi Gist's permission. Enraged, Gist gave the new husband 317 lashes on his bare back as a wedding present.

The severe beating destroyed Levin's health. Afterward, he had difficulty walking and seemed more and more like an old man to Peter. One day in 1831, Levin became very ill. By the time Peter reached the cabin his brother and Fanny shared, Levin was dead, at the age of thirty-three. In his heart, Peter grieved for his brother for the rest of his life, but he was not allowed to stop working for even a day. Because slaves weren't permitted to hold daytime funerals, Peter and Fanny buried Levin in an unmarked grave by torchlight, in the middle of the night.

A few years before his brother's death, Peter had met a fifteen-year-old girl from a neighboring plantation. Her name was Vina, and she had been born in North Carolina. As a child, Vina had seen her father led away in chains to be sold. Later, Vina had been separated from her mother and brothers and purchased by a planter named Bernard McKiernan. Peter was often sent on errands to the McKiernans', where he noticed a small, sad-eyed house slave staring at him. He asked her name and talked a little with her. Soon Vina began watching for Peter, just as he looked forward to seeing her. The two of them confessed their love for each other and decided to marry. Remembering how his brother had been whipped for marrying a girl "off the plantation," however, Peter delayed asking his master's permission.

One night while his master was away visiting relatives in Kentucky, Peter decided to follow his heart. He walked along the path to the McKiernan plantation and knocked on Vina's cabin door. They had a right to some happiness and should marry regardless of the consequences, he told Vina. A few days later they had a slave wedding. They pledged their mutual love, and a fellow slave who knew a little of the Bible blessed them with a few words.

Learning the news upon his return, Mr. Gist was angry, but he did not beat Peter as he had Levin for the same offense. At the close of each work week, Peter walked seven miles to spend Saturday night and Sunday with Vina. Since Vina shared a cabin with other slaves, Peter began building one of their own. He constructed the little house over many Sundays, sometimes working all through the night by moonlight and walking back at dawn on Monday to begin his new work week for Master Gist. Over the years, Peter and Vina had eight children. Four died in early childhood and one son drowned at the age of seventeen, but their sons Peter Junior and Levin and their daughter Catharine survived.

Peter was often reminded that he couldn't protect his family. When the couple's first child, Peter Junior, was a year old, Vina fought off an overseer who tried to rape her. The man struck Vina across the head, seriously injuring her. Peter wanted to kill the overseer, but that would have cost him his own life and probably result in his wife and son being sold. Fortunately, the overseer was fired and Vina recovered, although she was left with scars on her head.

One day when Peter Junior was about eight years old, he arrived in the yard a few minutes late for work because of a toothache. For this the boy was tied to an apple tree and given one hundred lashes. As the overseer whipped the child, Mr. McKiernan laughed and said, "That's the best way to cure a nigger's toothache." Again, Peter could only assure his family that one day things would be better.

Peter had been married five years when his owner, Levi Gist, died of a heart attack. Peter was thankful that he remained the property of Gist's relatives, because he could stay in the area, near his wife and children. He was hired out to a succession of people in and around Tuscumbia, so he was able to continue visiting his family on weekends. Over the years, Peter cleaned houses, picked cotton, made deliveries for stores, and worked as a janitor in a church and school.

Around 1844, the people Peter worked for began letting him run errands and do chores around Tuscumbia in his free time. Peter dug graves, carried pails of water, swept fireplaces, and blackened boots.

*A plantation slave family in South Carolina*

If there was an errand to run or a yard to rake, Tuscumbians called on "Uncle" Peter (older slaves were called "Uncle" and "Aunt," often condescendingly) to do the job. Vina sewed a leather purse for Peter in which he stored the dimes and quarters he received as tips. By the end of 1844, he had $15, and by 1846 about $100. The flame of hope, which had burned low for many years, was now rekindled. If he could save a few hundred dollars—and find a sympathetic owner—he might buy himself out of slavery and then find a way to rescue Vina and their children.

In 1847, Peter was hired out to work for Joseph and Isaac Friedman, brothers who ran a store in Tuscumbia. The Friedman brothers gave Peter clothes to take home to his family and paid him more for working in their store than he was required to hand over to his owners. By the end of the year, Peter had $210 in the purse his wife had made for him.

As he worked in the Friedmans' store, Peter began to think that at long last he had found white people he could trust. Not only were the Friedmans kind to him, but from their talk he could tell that they opposed slavery. Perhaps they hated persecution because they suffered it themselves. The Friedmans were the first Jewish people in the region. Tuscumbians liked to shop in the brothers' store and admitted that they charged fair prices. Yet behind their backs people said cruel things about them because of their religion.

Peter observed the Friedmans for more than a year before deciding to confide in Joseph, the older brother. At the end of a workday he followed the shopkeeper into the store's back room. "Mr. Friedman," he said, "I've got something I want to tell you—a great secret."

He had thought out what he would say a hundred times, but now that he was facing Mr. Friedman he hesitated. In 1834, Alabama had enacted a law discouraging white people from allowing slaves to buy their freedom. Suddenly the chances of Mr. Friedman agreeing to Peter's proposal seemed remote.

"Yes, Peter?" asked Mr. Friedman.

With his heart pounding and his knees trembling so that he could scarcely stand, Peter blurted out his plan. "I've been thinking, sir, I'd like to buy myself. And you've always dealt so fair with me, I didn't know but you might buy me, and then give me a chance to buy myself from you."

Joseph Friedman confessed that he had often wished Peter could be free, but had never thought of a way to accomplish it. "Yes, I will speak to Hogun," he said, referring to Peter's owner at that time, John Henry Hogun. Mr. Friedman added an idea of his own: Peter should pretend to have a terrible cough when he was near Hogun. This might convince his master that Peter was ill and should be sold while he still had some value.

The plan didn't work at first. The Friedman brothers couldn't convince Mr. Hogun to sell Peter. Peter spoke to him, too, making certain to cough, but his master wouldn't budge.

Another year passed. Then, in early 1849, something changed. John Henry Hogun wanted to buy a sixteen-year-old slave boy who was being auctioned, but he needed more cash. He approached Isaac Friedman (Joseph was in Texas on business) with a proposal. "Look here, Friedman," said Mr. Hogun. "You and your brother want Uncle Peter, and I want that boy who is for sale today. If you will go in and buy the boy for me, I will let you have Peter in exchange." Isaac Friedman wanted no part of a slave auction, but he countered with a similar proposal. He would pay $500 to buy Peter from Hogun, who could then use the money to bid on the young slave. Mr. Hogun agreed and drew up a bill of sale:

*For the consideration of five hundred dollars, paid to me this day, I have sold to Joseph [and Isaac] Friedman a negro man named Peter. Given under my hand and seal this 15th January, 1849.*

JOHN H. HOGUN

Peter spoke to his new owner in the back room of the store. Isaac Friedman explained that Peter must pay him and Joseph the $500 purchase price, for his liberation must appear to be strictly a business deal rather than a plot to free a slave. Furthermore, Peter should remain in Tuscumbia for a time, so that people would believe the Friedmans wanted him as a slave. In about a year, Isaac Friedman planned to go to Cincinnati, in the free state of Ohio, which would be a good place to liberate Peter.

Peter turned over all the money in his leather purse—$300—to Isaac Friedman. "You may work, as you have before," Isaac told him, "but you may keep your earnings. When you get two hundred dollars more, I will give you your free papers."

Shortly after Isaac Friedman bought him, Peter visited his wife and children and told them the wonderful news: In a year or so he would be free and up north, where he would arrange to free them, too.

Now allowed to keep all his earnings at the store, Peter quickly saved the $200 he still owed the Friedmans. In the spring of 1850, he paid off the last of his debt. That same day, Joseph Friedman wrote out what to Peter was the most precious document in the world: his free papers. Since Peter couldn't read, Joseph read him this:

*For, and in consideration of five hundred dollars, I have this 16th day of April, 1850, given Peter a Bill of Sale, and given him his freedom.*

*JOSEPH FRIEDMAN*
*Tuscumbia, Alabama, April 16th, 1850*

A few weeks later, the Friedmans sold their store. Joseph went to California to join the Gold Rush, while Isaac and Peter prepared to go to Cincinnati. Peter spent the last weekend before his departure with his family, telling them over and over how one day they would all live together as free people in the North. On Monday morning, when the bell rang summoning the slaves to work, Peter walked outside with Vina and their children. He held his wife's hand and promised her, "I will come back. I will come back for you!" Then Vina and the children went to work in the cotton fields, and Peter returned to Tuscumbia to get ready for his departure.

On July 20, 1850, Isaac Friedman and Peter left Tuscumbia by steamboat. Early on the morning of July 26, they arrived in Cincinnati. Ending fifty years of slavery, Peter leaped from the steamboat onto the free soil of Ohio and shouted, "I'm free! *I'm free!* This is free ground! The water runs free! The wind blows free! I am a slave no more!"

*Peter promising Vina that he will return for her and their children*

who came to his office for help. William hid his notes in a cemetery, where slave hunters couldn't find them. Later William retrieved his notes and turned them into his famous book, *The Underground Railroad.*

Peter asked William's advice about rescuing Vina and their three children from Alabama. The Anti-Slavery Society helped fugitives passing through Pennsylvania, William explained, and was not equipped to send people to liberate slaves in the South. Peter shocked William by announcing his intention to return to Alabama to rescue his family himself.

Not even his mother's pleadings could prevent Peter from setting off for Alabama, where he risked being forced back into slavery. Just a week after arriving in Philadelphia, Peter started his journey south. On the way, he stopped in Cincinnati and worked out a plan with Isaac Friedman. He then continued on to Tuscumbia, arriving on August 31.

People in Tuscumbia were curious about Peter's life in Cincinnati. He told them the story that he and Isaac Friedman had concocted: Although Ohio was free soil, he had remained with Isaac Friedman voluntarily as his slave, Peter said. Now Master Isaac had sent him down to Tuscumbia for a few weeks to earn money. In November, Peter would deliver his earnings to Master Isaac in Cincinnati. Then, before Christmas, master and slave would move back to Tuscumbia to reopen the store. Had it been known that he was actually free, Peter probably would have been arrested, but his story convinced the townspeople that he was still a slave. He resumed his former life, finding work as a school janitor and doing his usual odd jobs around town.

On the Saturday after his arrival in Tuscumbia, Peter went to visit his family on the McKiernan plantation, just as he had done when he was a slave. When he reached their cabin, he found Vina and their two sons and daughter cooking supper.

"Oh, Vina," Peter told his wife. "I've seen my mother! Vina, my mother is living, and I've got five brothers and three sisters!"

Peter remained in Tuscumbia for ten weeks. He earned $60 and visited Vina and their children several times, but he realized that he could not lead them to freedom himself. He told them that he would try to earn enough money up north to buy them out of slavery. However, he took Vina's gingham cape with him when he departed. If a rescuer came for them, Peter explained, the man would show her the cape as a sign that he was a friend.

Peter left Tuscumbia on November 13. Instead of returning to his "master," Isaac Friedman, he went to his brother William's home in Philadelphia, arriving on November 30, 1850. William had great news for Peter: A white man named Seth Concklin had offered to go down to Alabama to rescue Vina and the children. Peter gave Vina's cape to Concklin, who departed for the South in January 1851.

Nearly fifty years old, Concklin had hated slavery since his youth in New York State. He had helped fugitives escape on the UGRR, given much of his money to the abolitionist cause, and fought off a mob that tried to lynch a black man. Although he had been a soldier, Concklin set out unarmed from Philadelphia to rescue Peter's family, for he didn't want to shoot anyone. On a dark, cold night in late January, he reached the McKiernan plantation near the Tennessee River in northwestern Alabama.

Seth Concklin located Vina and spoke to her in a field. He pulled her cape from his pocket and gave it to her to prove that he was a friend. If Vina and the children would meet him by the river on a certain date, said Concklin, he would lead them to freedom by pretending to be a master taking his slaves on a trip.

While Peter's family prepared for the journey, Seth Concklin scouted the countryside and bought a small boat. On the night of March 15, 1851, Vina and the children met Concklin at a landing by the river. They climbed into his boat and began rowing northward, intending to travel more than a thousand miles to Windsor, Canada, where Peter would join them.

They made it halfway there. After surviving storms and barely avoiding being dashed to pieces by powerful winds, they reached Indiana. A few months earlier, the Fugitive Slave Law had gone into effect, so they were not safe in Indiana, even though it was a free state. They were inside a UGRR station—the home of a Quaker near Vincennes, Indiana—when seven armed slave hunters suddenly burst in and seized them. The slave catchers offered to let Seth Concklin go, but he insisted on riding in the wagon with Vina and her children to the Vincennes jail. Every day he visited them there, saying he would think of a way to free them.

"You can't do us any good, sir," Vina told him. "You'd best take care of yourself and get away." But Concklin remained in Vincennes, trying to think of a way to rescue the captured fugitives.

Soon a telegraph message from Bernard McKiernan in Alabama reached Vincennes. He described four slaves who had been stolen from him, offering four hundred dollars for their return plus six hundred dollars for the capture of the white man who had taken them away. With that, Concklin was seized and thrown in the Vincennes jail, too.

A few days later, McKiernan himself arrived to claim his slaves and return Seth Concklin to Alabama to face trial for slave stealing. On the way to Alabama, Concklin, whose hands and feet had been chained, drowned in the Ohio River. He may have been pushed off the vessel—killed as punishment for trying to rescue slaves.

Meanwhile, Peter was staying at his sister Mary's house in Philadelphia. Each day he looked forward to receiving word from Canada that his family was safe and that he should join them. One day Peter entered the parlor and found Mary reading a newspaper as tears rolled down her cheeks. "Oh, Peter," said Mary. "Have you heard the news?"

"No," he answered, for he could not yet read.

"Sit down and I will read it to you." Peter listened as Mary read a newspaper account of the capture of the four slaves and Seth Concklin. Not long after, word came of Concklin's death.

Peter was deeply discouraged. His wife and children had been whipped and returned to McKiernan's cotton fields. He was no closer to freeing them than he had been upon arriving in Philadelphia eight months earlier. But he had survived too many difficulties to give up. He decided to find out how much it would cost to buy Vina and their children out of slavery. Friends of his wrote to McKiernan asking his selling price.

McKiernan sent a reply to William Still in August 1851. Peter could buy his wife and children for $5,000. If Peter didn't raise that much money in three or four years, McKiernan would sell Vina and the children where he would never see them again.

All of Peter's relations together could not give him $5,000, which was equal to about $100,000 in today's money. William helped Peter get a job as a carriage driver and cook for a Burlington, New Jersey, family. His employers taught him to read and write. But even if he

# CHAPTER FIVE

# HENRY "BOX" BROWN AND LEAR GREEN

## *"Go and Get a Box and Put Yourself in It"*

*Escaped slaves often thought of ingenious places to hide. Nineteen-year-old John Thompson fled Alabama by riding on the roofs of train cars at night. Harry Grimes lived in the hollow of a large poplar tree in the North Carolina swamps for seven months before heading north. But a man and a woman who never met, Henry Brown and Lear Green, devised what were perhaps the most unusual hiding places.*

Henry Brown was born in Virginia in 1816. He was raised to be a house slave, running errands and waiting on his master and mistress. Henry's master tried to make his slaves obey him by telling them he was God. For example, whenever a storm approached he said they should run inside, for he was about to make it thunder. Soon after, the thunder would crash, as he had warned. He would then explain that he had made it rain to help the flowers and crops grow. Just as he had said, everything would look greener following the rainstorm. Henry's master also made vague promises that, if they obeyed him, his slaves would someday be free.

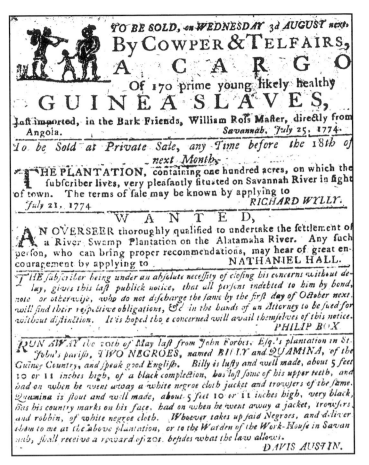

*Georgia advertisements from 1774*

One autumn day when Henry was about seven years old, his mother sat him on her lap and explained that their master was not God but an evil man who owned them and could sell them if he chose. She pointed to the trees and said, "Henry, as yonder leaves are stripped from the trees of the forests, so are the children of slaves swept away by the hands of cruel tyrants."

At the age of thirteen, Henry learned that his mother was right. His master, who was about to die, called Henry to his bedside. Instead of setting him free, he said, "Henry, you must be an honest boy, and never tell an untruth. I have given you to my son William, and you must obey him."

As Master William prepared to take Henry to Richmond, Virginia, to work in his tobacco factory, Henry's mother reminded him: "You now see, my son, the fulfillment of what I told you a great while ago, when I used to take you on my knee, and show you the leaves blown from the trees." Saying good-bye to his mother, Henry Brown realized that his master had been closer to the Devil than to God.

Master William did not run the tobacco factory himself. Instead, he employed an overseer, who kept the slaves hard at work by whipping them. Along with 120 other slaves, Henry spent fifteen hours a day in the factory, producing chewing tobacco.

After working a few years, Henry met a young woman named Nancy, who belonged to a bank clerk. Their friendship ripened into love, and they decided to marry—under one condition. Henry and Nancy both sought assurance that they would never be sold or otherwise separated. Their owners promised never to sell them, and Henry Brown and Nancy were married.

Although he was a slave, Henry was granted a small salary at the tobacco factory, while Nancy earned a few dollars a year taking in laundry. They rented a small house in Richmond, where they enjoyed as much happiness as slaves could have. During twelve years of marriage the couple had three children.

But the bank clerk broke his promise. Nancy was sold and then sold again—fortunately, to people in Richmond. Her newest owner told Henry that Nancy did not earn him enough money by taking in washing. He would sell her as a field slave, he threatened, unless Henry paid him a fee: $50 to start, and another $50 per year. That would protect Nancy from being sold away—or so Henry was led to believe.

On a pleasant morning in August 1848, Henry Brown left Nancy and their three children at home and went to the tobacco factory. Returning home for lunch, he found that his family was gone. A friend informed him that they were in prison. Nancy's owner had broken the agreement with Henry and had sold her and their three children to a North Carolina planter. They were being kept in prison until their departure the next day to prevent Henry from running off with them. If he visited the prison to see them, Henry was warned, he would be arrested.

Henry went to his own master and begged him to buy his family so that they could remain together. But his master refused, saying, "You can get another wife."

The next morning, Henry Brown waited by the side of the road along which his family would pass with several hundred other slaves who had been sold. He later described his feelings when he saw his wife and children go by:

*Pretty soon five wagonloads of little children passed, and looking at the [first] one, what should I see but a little child, pointing its tiny hand towards me, exclaiming: "There's my father. I knew he would come and bid me good-bye." It was my eldest child! Soon the gang approached in which my wife was chained. I looked, and beheld her familiar face. But O, reader, that glance of agony! May God spare me ever again enduring the excruciating horror of that moment! She passed, and came near to where I stood. I seized hold of her hand, intending to bid her farewell; but words failed me; the gift of utterance had fled, and I remained speechless. I followed her for some distance, with her hand grasped in mine, as if to save her from her fate, but I could not speak, and I was obliged to turn away in silence.*

From the moment that his family was led away, Henry Brown had a single purpose in life. He would escape to the North, learn where his family had been taken, and then raise money in order to buy them out of bondage.

To avoid arousing suspicion, Henry tried to act unconcerned over the loss of his family. He waited several months and then convinced the foreman of the tobacco factory to grant him some time off because of a badly injured finger. Actually, Henry had damaged the finger himself by pouring acid on it, which ate the skin away to the bone. While absent from work, Henry Brown formulated an escape plan. He never explained how it originated, for he didn't want to cause trouble for those who had helped him. All he would ever say was that while he was praying in despair God told him:

"Go and get a box and put yourself in it."

Henry visited the train depot, where he observed the size of the largest boxes in which merchandise was shipped. He then called on a carpenter friend (probably a free black man), and asked him to build a box three feet long, two feet wide, and two and a half feet deep, with three little holes in it. Guessing its purpose, the carpenter warned, "You cannot live inside it." Henry just thanked him and went on his way with the box.

Scattered about the South were a few white people who helped slaves escape. Assisting slaves was extremely risky, for southern planters hated white UGRR workers even more than they hated the fugitives themselves. But Henry Brown became acquainted with Samuel A. Smith, a white shoe dealer in Richmond, who promised to

*Henry "Box" Brown*

help him escape if Henry thought of a plan. One night Henry carried his box over to Smith's home.

"Is that to put your clothes in when you depart on your journey?" asked the shoe dealer.

"No, it is to put Henry Brown in!" he answered.

Smith was astonished when Brown explained his plan. Henry wanted to be enclosed in the box and then shipped to the North as if he were a load of shoes.

In March 1849, Henry climbed inside the box with a few biscuits and a container of water. Smith then nailed down the lid, on which THIS SIDE UP WITH CARE had been written. A friend or two of Smith's carried the box to the Adams Express Company office in Richmond. Smith telegraphed William Still to inform him that an important box would be arriving at the Adams Express office in Philadelphia at a certain time.

The box containing Henry Brown sat for a few minutes at the express company office before being taken to the train depot. Once the midnight train pulled into the station, the box was picked up and shoved into a baggage car. From inside his box, Henry heard the conductor ring the bell signaling departure and felt the wheels turning beneath him as the train chugged away.

As the hours passed, Henry grew faint. The three little holes didn't let in much air, and he was squashed into a doubled-up position that hardly allowed him to move. Things got worse when the train rolled to a stop and the box was moved onto a steamboat. The baggage handlers ignored the THIS SIDE UP label, and Henry Brown was placed with his head downward.

Soon his eyes felt as if they were popping out of their sockets, and the veins in his temples seemed about to burst. He broke out in a cold sweat from head to toe. Part of him wanted to cry out for help, but he vowed to himself that he would die rather than surrender. He remained upside down for about an hour and a half. Just when he thought that his head would explode, he overheard two crewmen approach and say, "Let us sit down and rest ourselves." They turned Henry's box right side up and sat on it for a few minutes before moving on.

Henry's head had just cleared when the steamer arrived in Washington, D.C. The box was loaded onto a wagon and taken to the train station, where it was thrown onto the platform. Fortunately the carpenter had done his job well and the box held together, but something cracked in Henry's neck when the crate landed. Henry heard a man say, "There is no room for this box. It will have to remain behind."

But then another voice ordered, "You will have to make room for it." The next thing Henry knew, he was thrown into the baggage car, once again landing upside down. At one of the first stops after Washington, D.C., more baggage had to be loaded onto the car and, in the process, the box was turned to the proper position. Henry arrived in Philadelphia in the middle of the night, after a twenty-six-hour journey.

His ordeal wasn't over. There was confusion about the box's arrival time. William Still went to the Adams Express office in Philadelphia at two-thirty in the morning—on the day *before* Henry Brown was to arrive. He looked around but didn't see any box for William Johnson, as Samuel A. Smith had informed him it would be addressed. Later that day, William Still received a telegram from Smith saying "Your case of goods is shipped and will arrive tomorrow morning."

William Still thought that it might look suspicious if he returned to look over the boxes the next morning, so he sent a carriage driver to fetch the box. But he did not tell him that a man was inside. The driver didn't pick up the box until six in the morning, with the result that Henry spent an extra three hours sitting in the express company office, not knowing whether anyone would ever come to get him.

Finally, Henry felt himself being lifted into a wagon. He was delivered to a building where he heard men talking about him as though they thought he was dead. One of them gave the signal that Samuel A. Smith had arranged, rapping on the lid and calling out, "Is all right within?"

Instantly, Henry Brown replied, "All right, sir!"

Using a saw and a hatchet, William Still and three fellow abolitionists removed the lid. Up stood Henry Brown. He tried to maintain a brave front, holding out his hand and saying, "How do you do, gentlemen?" but he was so exhausted from his journey that he fainted.

He awoke to find William Still and the three other men hovering over him. In honor of the fugitive's unusual means of escape, Still nicknamed him "Box" Brown.

Although his neck was not seriously injured, Henry Box Brown needed a few days to recover his strength. He stayed in William Still's house and with the family of Lucretia Mott, an abolitionist also known for her work on behalf of women's rights. William Still then sent him on to Boston, Massachusetts, a safer place for runaway slaves. Brown became a popular lecturer in Massachusetts and Maine as people flocked to hear him describe his escape. With the help of an abolitionist friend, he wrote the story of his life, *Narrative of Henry Box Brown*, which was published in 1849, the same year he made his journey to freedom.

Henry did not forget why he had fled slavery. Soon after his arrival in Boston, he asked abolitionists to write letters for him asking about the whereabouts of his wife and children. Their new owner, in North Carolina, informed him that he could buy them for $1,200. However, it appears that Brown was never able to free his family. And in the summer of 1850, slave catchers nearly kidnapped him. To put himself beyond the reach of the new Fugitive Slave Law, Box Brown fled to England. He told his story in Great Britain for a few years, but disappeared from history in the mid-1850s.

Meanwhile, in Richmond, Samuel A. Smith had decided to help more slaves by shipping them north in crates. Shortly after Henry Brown's successful escape, two slaves whom Smith had assisted were discovered in their boxes and returned to bondage. Smith was arrested and sent to the Richmond penitentiary. In prison, he was stabbed near the heart by a proslavery man, but survived.

Upon his release from prison after seven years, Smith gave a

*Henry Box Brown emerging from his crate in the Pennsylvania Anti-Slavery Society office; William Still is holding the lid.*

speech in Philadelphia. He told the audience that, despite all he had suffered, he rejoiced in having helped Henry Box Brown and others achieve their liberty.

Because of his book and his colorful nickname, Henry Box Brown was the most famous slave to escape in a crate. But similar escapes

Aboard the vessel, Mrs. Adams was told that, although she was free, she could not travel in a cabin. All black passengers had to remain out on the deck. This actually suited her, for she could stand next to the chest containing Lear and watch over it without arousing suspicion.

All night Lear remained cramped in the chest, suffering from the heat and barely able to breathe. Once or twice during the night, Mrs. Adams loosened the ropes holding the chest closed and lifted the lid slightly to check on Lear. Each time Lear assured her that she was all right.

*Lear Green in her box*

Eighteen hours after Lear Green had climbed into her hiding place, the steamer arrived at the Philadelphia wharves. The chest was taken to a friend of Mrs. Adams, who directed her to continue on to the residence of William Still.

Still had been present when Henry Brown was delivered, but he may have been even more astonished when the ropes were untied and a young black woman climbed out of the chest. "Lear Green won for herself a strong claim to a high place among the heroic women of the nineteenth century," he later wrote—high praise from a man who had aided hundreds of escaped slaves.

Lear Green remained with William Still's family for several days. In case anyone was pursuing her and Mrs. Adams, Still arranged for them to be forwarded by the Underground Railroad to Elmira, New York, where Mrs. Adams seems to have made her home. Meanwhile, William Adams had left Baltimore; he arrived in Elmira at about the same time as Lear. Soon after being reunited in the free state of New York, Lear and William Adams were married.

For three years, Lear and her husband lived happily in Elmira. Then, when Lear was only about twenty-one years old, she died—of what is not known. Whether she left any children behind is also unknown, but it is known that she spent her last years as she had wanted: with her husband, as a free person. For the rest of his life, William Still kept the chest Lear Green had escaped in, as a memorial to the young woman he had greatly admired.

# CHAPTER SIX

# ELLEN AND WILLIAM CRAFT

### *"A Desperate Leap for Liberty"*

*Sometimes, slaves tried to escape by changing their appearance. Occasionally, fugitive slaves painted their skin white. Now and then, white abolitionists painted their faces black, in order to lure slave hunters into chasing them instead of the real fugitives. And a number of slaves tried to escape by wearing disguises. One of the most remarkable of these stories is of a young slave couple from Macon, Georgia.*

The stars still twinkled above their one-room cabin when Ellen and William Craft awoke before dawn on December 21, 1848. Anyone peeking through their window on that winter morning would have seen a strange sight as the shivering couple moved about by candlelight. First, William cut off most of Ellen's hair with scissors. He then dressed in his usual work clothes, adding one extra touch—a fancy beaver hat. Meanwhile, Ellen began dressing in an elegant man's suit.

She stepped into the trousers and buttoned the shirt. Her husband helped her with the necktie, boots, and black jacket. Next came green-tinted glasses to cover her eyes, a "toothache handkerchief" to hide her smooth cheeks, and a sling over her right arm. After she put on a top hat to complete her costume, her husband nodded in approval. "You make a most respectable-looking gentleman," he told her.

The Crafts were about to attempt one of the longest and most daring escapes ever made by slaves—a thousand-mile journey from Macon, Georgia, to Philadelphia, Pennsylvania. Ellen, who was a light-skinned black woman, was posing as a rich white planter going north for his health. William, who was dark, was pretending to be the young gentleman's slave.

As the stars faded from the sky, Ellen and William embraced for what might be the last time, for if they were caught they would probably be sold apart. William raised the door latch and glanced outside. Nothing stirred except the trees swaying in the early-morning breeze. "Come, my dear," William whispered, "let us make a desperate leap for liberty."

Once outside, they walked to the train station, taking different routes. William arrived first. He placed their suitcase in the baggage compartment, boarded the train's "Negro car," and pulled his hat down low to hide his face. Soon after, Ellen walked up to the ticket window and in her deepest voice asked for tickets for "William Johnson and slave" to travel to Savannah, Georgia, two hundred miles from Macon. Ellen then took a seat in a "whites only" car, relieved that, so far, no one had questioned "Mr. Johnson"'s identity.

⎯⎯⊰⊱⎯⎯

When they fled, the Crafts were both twenty-two years old. They had been slaves in Georgia their entire lives.

Ellen had been born in Clinton, Georgia, in 1826. Her father, a wealthy white planter named Major James Smith, was also her

*Portrait of Ellen Craft*

owner—a common situation on southern plantations. Ellen's mother was a house slave named Maria.

Because the sons and daughters of slave women were automatically slaves from birth, planters could increase their wealth by fathering children among their female slaves. Major Smith owned a hotel and plantation in Clinton and approximately a hundred slaves, including Maria. When Maria was about seventeen years old, Major Smith broke into her cabin and raped her. The major was pleased when Maria gave birth to Ellen, a fine-looking baby worth several hundred dollars.

Ellen grew up very close to her mother. Together they sewed, cooked, washed clothes, and cleaned Major and Mrs. Smith's plantation house. But Maria warned Ellen that she must call Major

*Ellen Craft in her costume*

Smith "Master," never "Father," for he viewed the girl as just another of his slaves. While she craved a little attention from her father, Ellen wished that the major's wife would leave her alone. No matter how carefully Ellen dusted the furniture or washed the floors, Mrs. Smith found fault and yelled at her or boxed her ears. The worst times were when visitors stopped by. Because of Ellen's light complexion and close resemblance to her father, many people assumed she was Mrs. Smith's daughter. Visitors sometimes even remarked that Ellen was the prettiest of the Smith children. Then Mrs. Smith would turn red and explain that Ellen was her *slave,* not her daughter. Once her guests left, she would fly into a rage and whip Ellen.

Ellen was too young to understand that Mrs. Smith resented her because she was a living reminder of the major's unfaithfulness. A slave herself, Maria could not protect her daughter from the blows. She could only comfort Ellen by pointing out their blessings. While the other slaves toiled in the cotton fields, didn't they work in the Smiths' mansion, wear the Smiths' discarded clothing, and eat scraps off the Smiths' plates? And while other slave families were torn apart, didn't Maria and Ellen live together?

But Mrs. Smith found a way to get rid of Ellen. In April 1837, the Smiths' daughter, Eliza, married Dr. Robert Collins of Macon. Mrs. Smith gave Ellen to her daughter as a wedding present. Following the ceremony, eleven-year-old Ellen was dragged from her mother and

*A rare photograph of William Craft*

forced into the newlyweds' carriage. The Collinses took her to Macon, where, like a real-life Cinderella, she became her half-sister's maid, cooking and cleaning for her, much as her mother did for the Smiths in Clinton. A year after the wedding, Major and Mrs. Smith also moved to Macon, bringing Ellen's mother with them. Ellen and her mother were then reunited—at least on Sundays, when they were issued passes so that they could walk through the woods or stroll through Macon, looking in the store windows.

As she grew older, Ellen displayed a gift for sewing. She sewed clothing for the Collinses and their children, and was hired by families in Macon to do the same for them. She had to turn over most of her earnings to her owners, but she was permitted to keep a little for herself. Ellen served her half-sister so faithfully that, when she was about sixteen, she was allowed to move into her own small cabin in the woods behind the Collins mansion.

About two years later, Ellen met William Craft, a young man whose life as a slave had been more difficult than hers. Born somewhere in Georgia, William came from a large, loving family that worked in the cotton fields. But when Mr. Craft, their master, needed money, William's parents were sold to different owners, never to see each other again. Next, Mr. Craft sold William's two brothers and one of his sisters. Finally, only William and his sister Sarah remained together, but when he was sixteen and she fourteen, they, too, were taken to the slave market and offered for sale.

Sarah was led to the auction block first. William watched in anguish while the bidders examined his sister as though she were a racehorse. A planter who lived far out in the countryside made the highest offer for Sarah. Watching his sister being led away in the planter's cart, William fell to his knees and begged to be allowed to bid her farewell, but the auctioneer pulled him to his feet by his neck. Forevermore, William was haunted by the memory of his sister staring after him with tears pouring down her cheeks.

William was then bought by a Macon banker named Taylor, who considered him a great investment. A talented carpenter, William was put to work in a Macon cabinet shop. Mr. Taylor received most of William's pay while spending little for his upkeep, for William found a night job waiting tables at a hotel in exchange for meals and a place to sleep. Working about a hundred hours a week, William gradually saved a little money from his tips at the hotel and the portion of his cabinet shop salary that he was allowed to keep.

Soon after they met, Ellen and William fell in love, but for a time she refused to marry him. Both of them came from families that had been separated, and Ellen was afraid the same thing would happen to them. Love finally overcame her fears. A fellow slave pronounced them husband and wife, and William moved from the hotel into Ellen's cabin on the Collins estate.

Horrified by the prospect of having their children taken from them and sold, the couple decided to remain childless unless they could escape. They often discussed that subject. Despite being unable to read or write, they had some idea of geography and knew that most successful slave escapes were from states near the North, such as Maryland, Virginia, and Kentucky. Escaping from a state in the Deep South, like Georgia, was overwhelmingly difficult, for it involved traveling hundreds of miles through forests, mountains, and snake-filled swamps. William and Ellen had seen captured runaways branded with red-hot irons and even tortured to death.

In late 1848, William suggested an odd plan. If they disguised Ellen as a suntanned white planter heading to the North with his slave, they could travel by train and steamboat rather than attempt the almost impossible journey on foot. The scheme might work, William argued, because Ellen was light-skinned and had served as her half-sister's maid for so long that she spoke like a wealthy white southerner. At first, Ellen considered the idea ridiculous, but William kept trying to persuade her. He asked her if, in two years of marriage, they had ever thought of a better plan. Didn't she want to have children and raise them in freedom?

Her husband's talk about raising a family silenced her objections. "If you purchase the disguise, I will try to carry out the plan," Ellen told him.

William took some of their savings and visited various stores in Macon. Although slaves were supposed to have a note from their owners to buy things in stores, shopkeepers commonly ignored this law. At one store, William bought a man's top hat and also a fancy beaver hat, such as a wealthy gentleman's personal slave might wear. Elsewhere he bought a gentleman's coat, boots, and other clothing. As William made these purchases, Ellen sewed herself a pair of men's trousers.

When Ellen first tried on the costume, her beardless face clearly revealed that she was a woman. Besides, if they left without permission, their owners might send slave hunters after them within a few hours. And what would Ellen do if, along the way, "Mr. Johnson" was asked to sign his name?

But Ellen was now committed to the plan, and she refused to give up. She sent William to make another purchase, a pair of green-shaded spectacles. With the glasses and the toothache handkerchief to hide her face, people wouldn't see her pretty eyes and smooth skin. At Christmastime, slave owners often issued passes to trusted slaves so that they could visit relatives and friends for a few days. Ellen persuaded her half-sister to write her a pass. The cabinetmaker who employed William gave him one, too. Both Crafts were ordered to return within a week—by which time they hoped to be in Pennsylvania.

But what about Ellen's inability to write? One night as they pondered this problem, Ellen said, "I think I have it!" They would bind her arm in a sling, as though she suffered from arthritis. This would provide her with an excuse for not being able to sign her name.

They hid the costume in a chest of drawers that William had built for Ellen. At dawn, four days before Christmas of 1848, they set out on their "desperate leap for liberty."

As Ellen and William sat waiting for their train to depart, their worst nightmare seemed about to come true. The cabinetmaker for whom William worked had become suspicious of him. At the last moment, he came running along the platform and began looking in the train windows. Just as he approached the Negro car, the conductor rang the bell and the train chugged out of the station.

Meanwhile, in Ellen's car, a friend of the Collinses named Mr. Cray sat next to her. Ellen's heart beat wildly, for Mr. Cray had known her since she was a child. Only a day earlier, she had served him dinner.

"It is a very fine morning, sir," Mr. Cray said. Certain that he would recognize her voice, Ellen pretended to be deaf and continued to stare out the window. "It is a very fine morning, sir!" Mr. Cray shouted. Unable to ignore him any longer, Ellen answered yes in a low voice, without looking his way. Mr. Cray gave up trying to make conversation, but Ellen scarcely breathed until he stepped off the train at a nearby town.

The train chugged along at about twenty miles per hour. In their separate cars, Ellen and William watched Georgia's red clay hills, pine woods, swamplands, and cotton and rice fields roll by. Around early evening they arrived in Savannah, where they left the train and climbed into a carriage. Once they reached the waterfront, Ellen bought tickets for "William Johnson and slave" to take the steamboat to Charleston, South Carolina.

"Mr. Johnson" was shown to a cabin on the vessel. However, William was told there was no place for black passengers to sleep. He paced the deck most of the night, sleeping for an hour or two on some bags of cotton near the boat's funnel.

By morning, William was weak with hunger. Mr. Johnson brought his slave to the breakfast table with him, explaining that because of his crippled arm he required assistance. The other passengers shook their heads disapprovingly when Mr. Johnson thanked his slave for cutting his food and let him eat scraps off his plate. "Nothing spoils a slave more than saying thank you to him," advised a young southern army officer. "The way to make a nigger toe the mark is to storm at him like thunder!" He demonstrated by cursing fiercely at his own slave for no reason. A slave dealer at the table warned Mr. Johnson that William looked as if he would run away once he reached the North. "Mention your price, and I will buy him from you with hard silver dollars," the slave dealer offered.

Men like this had been selling their people for generations, but Ellen couldn't afford to lose her temper. "I don't wish to sell him, sir," she said. "I cannot get on well without him."

Soon after, the vessel docked at Charleston, a major slave market with strict rules about taking black people through the city. The Crafts entered the steamship office, where Mr. Johnson asked to buy two tickets to transport himself and his slave by steamboat and train to Philadelphia.

"Boy, do you belong to this gentleman?" the port official behind the counter demanded of William. After William said he did, the official shoved a ledger book onto the counter and told Mr. Johnson, "Register your name here, and the name of your nigger, and pay a dollar duty on him."

Mr. Johnson paid the dollar but, pointing to his crippled arm, asked the official to sign for him. The man looked at him suspiciously and said he must sign for himself, using his left hand, if need be. As passengers waiting in line behind them told them to hurry up, Ellen and William stared at each other helplessly. Just when they thought they were trapped, the soldier who had advised Mr. Johnson to "storm at" his slave approached the counter. He shook hands with Mr. Johnson and told the official that he would vouch for him. Because the army officer was well known in Charleston, the Crafts were allowed to proceed.

Farther and farther north the fugitives traveled. They went by steamboat up the coast to Wilmington, North Carolina. There they changed to a train. When it crossed into Virginia, they were halfway through their thousand-mile journey. But they were now on their third day of travel with little sleep or food, and they were finding it difficult to remain alert.

When they changed trains at Richmond, Virginia, a plump elderly woman sat next to Ellen. As William walked along the platform to the Negro car, the woman said, "Bless my soul, there goes my nigger, Ned!"

"No, he is *my* boy!" protested Mr. Johnson, but the woman stuck her head out the window and ordered, "You, Ned! Come to me, you runaway rascal!"

When William turned around, the woman apologized to Mr. Johnson. "I never in my life saw two black pigs more alike than your boy and my Ned," she said. "I was as kind to Ned as if he had been my own son, but he ran off without any cause whatever."

Had she not been so tired, Ellen might not have asked why Ned had run away. The woman bragged that she had overturned the will of her husband, who, on his deathbed, had declared all his slaves free. "He wasn't in his right mind," she said. She further explained that Ned had gone off to search for his wife, whom she had sold to a New Orleans slave dealer. Fuming, Ellen called the woman "unkind," angering her and attracting the attention of other passengers. But instantly Ellen realized that her outburst had endangered William and herself. Ellen said nothing further, letting the woman rant on about "ungrateful niggers who run away."

Ellen and William left the train near Fredericksburg, Virginia, and continued by steamboat up the Potomac River to Washington, D.C. A fellow passenger, a planter, tried to pick a fight with Mr. Johnson. "You are spoiling your nigger by letting him wear such a devilish fine hat," said the planter. "I'd like to kick it overboard and sell every damned nigger dressed like a white man way down South, where the Devil would be whipped out of them!" Ellen had learned her lesson from her encounter with the old lady. She glared at the man and then walked away, leaving him cursing to himself.

A few minutes later, the steamer pulled in at Washington. As a carriage took them to the train station, the couple observed that the nation's capital was decked out in its holiday finery, for it was Christmas Eve.

After a two-hour train ride, they arrived in Baltimore, Maryland. Now all that remained was to change to one more train. Forty miles to the north, that train would cross the border to the most glorious spot on earth: the free-soil state of Pennsylvania. The

Crafts were so exhausted and excited that they had trouble walking along the platform. William helped Ellen onto the Philadelphia-bound train. Then, just as William was stepping into the Negro car, a station official rapped him on the shoulder and demanded, "Where are you going, boy?"

"To Philadelphia, sir," William answered. "I am traveling with my master, who is in the next carriage, sir."

"Get him out mighty quick!" ordered the official. "It is against the rules to take a slave past here, unless your master can prove in the office his right to do so."

William stepped into Ellen's car to explain the situation. Stunned by the bad news, she whispered, "Good heavens, William, is it possible that we are doomed to bondage after all?"

Trying to appear calm, the couple walked to the station office. The man in charge explained that Mr. Johnson had to prove that he wasn't helping someone else's slave escape, for abolitionists often tried to sneak fugitives through Baltimore to the free state of Pennsylvania. Did Mr. Johnson have papers showing that he owned William? He had left them at home, Mr. Johnson answered. "Well, sir," said the official, "then I can't let you go."

Ellen and William realized that their future depended upon what she said next. Staring icily at the official through her green glasses, Ellen said, in a commanding voice, "I bought tickets in Charleston to pass us through to Philadelphia! You have no right to detain us here!"

The bell rang, signaling that the train was about to depart. As everyone in the office looked on, the official hesitated, then quietly said, "As you are not well, it is a pity to stop you here. We will let you go."

Ellen and William rushed to the platform and boarded the train

*Poster warning black Bostonians following the passage of the Fugitive Slave Law*

just before it rolled out of the station. They were so weary that they both fell asleep in their separate cars. Sometime in the night the train crossed into Pennsylvania. Toward dawn, they awoke to the sound of the train whistle and looked out their windows at the lights of Philadelphia. Even before the wheels stopped turning, William dashed into Ellen's car.

"Thank God, William," Ellen said, as they traveled by carriage to a boardinghouse on that Christmas morning. "We are free!"

As news of the Crafts' escape spread, Philadelphia abolitionists, including William Still, came to meet them and offer help. The couple's new friends feared that slave hunters might seize them in Philadelphia, so for three weeks Ellen and William stayed with a

Christmas 1850, almost exactly two years after leaving their little cabin in Macon.

They had traveled five thousand miles and were free at last.

———◦———

The Crafts lived in England for nearly twenty years. They attended school, ran a boardinghouse, and wrote a book titled *Running a Thousand Miles for Freedom,* which described their escape to Philadelphia. The couple bought a home in a London suburb, where they raised a family, which eventually included a daughter, four sons, and three adopted boys from Africa.

Back in the United States, the Civil War ended in 1865. Thousands of former fugitive slaves returned to the South as free people. Among them were the Crafts, who settled near Savannah and opened a school for poor people on their farm. Eventually Mrs. Craft's School, as it was called, had about a hundred pupils.

In later life, Ellen and William Craft became known for their kind deeds. They paid for the weddings of needy young couples and took medicine to sick neighbors. Surrounded by their family, the couple lived happily for many years. But instead of telling their grandchildren fairy tales, they told the true story of how, a long time ago, they had made "a desperate leap for liberty."

# CHAPTER SEVEN

# WILLIAM WELLS BROWN
## *"Now Try to Get Your Liberty!"*

*It is a little-known fact that five thousand black men fought to free the United States from England during the American Revolution (1775–83). Some were free blacks, but others were slaves who were promised their liberty once the war was won. Sadly, these promises were often broken, and many black soldiers who helped liberate their country from England were returned to slavery after the war ended. Such was the fate of Simon Lee, a Virginia slave who bravely served in the Revolution, only to be sent back to his master's plantation to spend the rest of his life in bondage. And because Simon remained a slave, his descendants for several generations were born into slavery, including his grandson William Wells Brown.*

Simon had a daughter named Elizabeth, who was taken from Virginia to Kentucky as a child. Elizabeth worked in the tobacco fields on the plantation of Dr. John Young, a prominent physician and farmer in the Lexington, Kentucky, region. Dr. Young "lent" some of his female slaves to his male relatives, so that they could rape them. This happened to Elizabeth, who had seven children with seven different fathers. Elizabeth's son William, born around 1814, never knew his father, who was Dr. Young's brother.

When William was two years old, Dr. and Mrs. Young moved with their forty slaves to Missouri, where Dr. Young practiced medicine and grew tobacco. Perhaps because he was the doctor's nephew, William was raised as a house slave, which was considered a privilege. William's mother, however, was a field slave and was expected to be at work by four-thirty in the morning. One of William's first memories was of awakening to the sound of his mother's cries as the

*William Wells Brown*

overseer whipped her for arriving in the field ten minutes late. Listening to her screams, William trembled in helpless fury. As he later wrote, "Nothing is more heart-rending than to see a beloved mother or sister tortured, and to hear their cries, and not be able to render them assistance."

A few years later, Dr. and Mrs. Young adopted a white nephew of theirs, who was also named William. Having two Williams in the house was confusing, so Dr. Young told the young slave that he was changing his name. Henceforth William the slave would be Sandford. But the young boy persisted in calling himself William, for which he was whipped. To make things worse, William was required not only to do his chores around the house but also to baby-sit and wait on little William, who was actually his cousin.

Dr. Young was elected to the Missouri legislature, so he often had to be away from home for long periods. His overseer, Grove Cook, ran the farm in his absence. Cook sent William out to the tobacco fields and whipped him for not working fast enough. On one occasion, he punished William by making him get down on his hands and knees in front of a large ram in the sheep pasture. The animal butted the boy in the forehead with his horns, sending him flying. As blood gushed from William's head, the overseer enjoyed a hearty laugh and sent him back to work.

In 1827, when William was thirteen, the Youngs moved to a farm near St. Louis, Missouri. William's family was quickly broken apart. Two of his brothers died. Dr. Young sold William's only sister and his three remaining brothers. The doctor also decided that William and his mother, Elizabeth, would be more profitable to him if he hired them out to work in St. Louis. Elizabeth was hired out for a short time and then purchased by a St. Louis tinsmith. Over the next few years

William worked as a tavern keeper's helper, a hotel keeper's servant, an errand boy for the *St. Louis Times,* and a waiter and barber on a Mississippi River steamboat.

William had plenty of chances to run away while working at these jobs, but he also had a compelling reason to stay: Now and then he was allowed to visit his mother and his sister, both of whom were still in the St. Louis area. Despite the lure of freedom, he couldn't bear to leave them behind and perhaps never see them again.

A man named James Walker had observed William working on the steamboat and was impressed with him. In 1832, Walker paid Dr. Young a huge sum—$900—to rent eighteen-year-old William for a year. It was the worst year of William's life, for Walker was a buyer and seller of slaves—what white people called a "Negro speculator" and black people called a "soul driver." William accompanied Walker up and down the Mississippi River as the dealer purchased slaves and then sold them at a profit. One of William's tasks was to pluck out the gray hairs of elderly slaves and dye their hair black to make them look younger.

William witnessed many instances of James Walker's cruelty, but one incident was especially horrifying. While they were marching a group of slaves along a road, a sick baby traveling in his mother's arms began to cry. "Stop the child's damned noise—or *I* will!" Walker warned the mother. That night they stayed in a boardinghouse. The next morning, as they prepared to leave, the infant began crying again. Walker grabbed the baby from his mother and, ignoring her pleas, gave the child to the boardinghouse landlady. "Madam, I make you a present of this little nigger," he told the white woman. "It makes such a noise that it affects my nerves."

"Thank you, sir," said the woman, accepting the gift.

A few days later, while the slaves were on the steamboat heading to the New Orleans slave market, the mother leaped from the deck into the Mississippi River and drowned herself.

After serving Mr. Walker for a year, William returned to Dr. Young, who had sad news for him. William's sister had been sold to a man from Natchez, Mississippi. Dr. Young was short of money and so William must be sold, too. But since William was his nephew, Dr. Young would do him a favor. William could go into St. Louis and find someone to buy him. All Young wanted was $500 from the sale.

"Do you not call me a good master?" asked Dr. Young, who thought it was generous of him to let William sell himself.

"No," William replied angrily, talking back to his master for the first time in his life. "If you were, you would not sell us."

William set out with instructions to return in a week with some-one who would pay Dr. Young at least $500 for him. Once in St. Louis, he learned that his sister had not yet departed. She was being held in jail for safekeeping until her new owner was ready to take her to Mississippi.

The jailer turned William away several times before allowing him to visit his sister for a few minutes. William found her in a cell with four other women, all purchased by the same man. The moment she saw William she threw her arms around his neck and burst into tears. She had time for only a few parting words. "There is no hope for me— I must live and die a slave," she told him. "But you take Mother and leave slavery." Unable to do anything else for her, William removed a ring from his finger and gave it to his sister as a farewell gift. As he left the jail, he made up his mind to follow his sister's advice and take their mother to Canada.

He visited his mother and begged her to flee with him. At first, she refused, saying, "You go if you can, but as all my children are in slavery, I do not wish to leave them." William persisted and finally persuaded her to run off with him the next night.

The following day, William bought some dried beef, cheese, and crackers with a little money he had saved from his various jobs. He also explored the riverfront, finding an isolated spot where a small boat was docked.

William and his mother set out at nine o'clock that night for the waterfront where William had seen the boat. Using a board as an oar, he paddled the two of them to the Illinois shore. Mother and son then headed into the woods.

For more than a week they made their way through Illinois. Each night they emerged from the woods and traveled quietly along the roads. If they weren't sure which way to go, they looked toward the fugitive slave's guiding light—the North Star—which William later said became their "friend and leader."

On the eighth day of their journey they were drenched by a downpour. Two days later they ran out of food and decided to take a chance by stopping at a farmhouse. Fortunately, the family inside befriended the runaways, who now learned that they had traveled 150 miles from St. Louis. The farm family fed them and provided them with dry clothing and a place to sleep.

Thinking that they weren't likely to encounter slave hunters so far from home, the fugitives decided to continue their journey by daylight. In the morning the family packed some food for them. William and his mother thanked their hosts and resumed their flight northward.

As they walked along a quiet road, William told his mother how, once they were in Canada, he would buy a little farm for the two of

*Fugitive slaves escaping*

them and earn enough money to buy his sister and brothers out of bondage. They were discussing their happy future when suddenly three men on horseback rode up and ordered them to halt.

"What do you want?" William boldly demanded, hoping to convince the men that he and his mother were free blacks.

One of the men pulled a handbill out of his pocket and read it aloud. Issued by Dr. Young and the St. Louis tinsmith who owned Elizabeth, it described the two runaways and offered a $200 reward for their return. The slave catchers tied William with a rope, shoved him and his mother into a wagon, and returned them to St. Louis, where they were locked in separate jail cells.

After a week in jail, William was taken to Dr. Young, who seemed disappointed that he had run away despite his "kindness" in allowing the young slave to choose a new master. Because of a promise he had made to his brother, explained Dr. Young, he would not ship William to a Deep South cotton plantation, the usual fate of captured runaways. Instead, he sent William out to work in his fields, telling his overseer to whip William for running away and to lock him up every night so he couldn't escape again.

Two or three weeks later, Dr. Young visited St. Louis. He returned with the news that he had sold William for $500 to a tailor in the city. This pleased William, for his mother was still in jail in St. Louis, awaiting her owner's decision about what to do with her.

The tailor—who wouldn't have allowed this had he known that William had run away—put him to work doing odd jobs around St. Louis. William soon discovered that his mother's owner had decided to ship her down to New Orleans for sale at that city's slave market. He visited the jail and begged to see Elizabeth before she was sent away, but the jailer suspected he would attempt to rescue her and refused to admit him. William then learned the name of the steamboat on which she would be traveling. On the morning of its departure, he boarded the vessel and found his mother in chains with fifty or sixty other slaves. "She moved not, neither did she weep," he later wrote. "Her emotions were too deep for tears."

Falling to his knees, William begged his mother to forgive him for convincing her to run away. "My dear son," she said soothingly, "you are not to blame for my being here. My Heavenly Master will soon call me home, and then I shall be out of the hands of the slaveholders!" Just then her owner, the tinsmith, saw them talking together. "My child," his mother quickly whispered in William's ear, "you have said that you would not die a slave. Now try to get your liberty!"

The tinsmith ran up to William and gave him a ferocious kick.

"Leave here this instant," he ordered. "You have been the cause of my losing one hundred dollars to get this wench back!"

As William left the steamboat, his mother cried out, "God be with you!" These were her last words to William, for he never saw her again. He stood on shore and watched as the vessel bearing his mother steamed down the river.

Soon after, William went to work for Enoch Price, a steamboat captain, who bought him from the tailor for $700. William was to wait on passengers on Captain Price's steamboats and also drive the Price family's carriage part of the time. At first, William was so stunned by losing his mother that he didn't think of escaping, but her parting words gradually sank in: "Now try to get your liberty!" The best way to do that, he decided, was to act obedient while awaiting his opportunity.

In December 1833, the Prices traveled to New Orleans aboard their steamer, the *Chester*. William, now almost twenty years old, was taken along as the family servant. After vacationing with his family for a few days in New Orleans, Captain Price had an opportunity to mix business with pleasure. He took on a load of cargo to be delivered to Cincinnati, Ohio. William had been so polite and obedient during his three months with him that Captain Price wasn't concerned about taking him into the free state of Ohio.

The *Chester* arrived in Cincinnati late on December 31, 1833. The next day, while the cargo was being unloaded, William walked off the vessel carrying someone's trunk, as if his master had ordered him to take it ashore. He walked up the street and disappeared into a marshy woodland, where he remained until the sun went down. It was New Year's Day, and William hoped that in a week or two he would be in Canada, starting a new life.

"Then I will call thee William Wells Brown," said the man. The fugitive departed from the Quaker couple with the name that was his ever after.

In about a week, William Wells Brown reached Cleveland but found that he couldn't sail to Canada until the spring because Lake Erie was frozen. He could have gone around the lake to Canada, but, feeling that he was beyond the grasp of slave hunters, he remained in Cleveland.

He knocked on doors, offering to work as a handyman in exchange for food and a place to sleep. One family hired him to saw firewood for a quarter, which he spent on a spelling book and a bag of candy. He asked the family's two little boys to teach him to read, paying them for each lesson with a little candy. A few weeks later, a Cleveland hotel hired him as a waiter, providing him with his own room and paying him a salary of $12 a month.

In the spring, Brown went to work on a Lake Erie steamboat and began his career as an UGRR conductor. His work on steamers over the next few years enabled him to transport many fugitive slaves to Canada, including sixty-nine in a single year. William met and married Elizabeth Schooner in 1834. Two years later, the couple moved to Buffalo, New York, where they turned their home into an UGRR station. The marriage didn't work out, though, and in 1847, after separating from Elizabeth, William Wells Brown took his two young daughters to Boston, which became his permanent home.

William Wells Brown fought slavery on many fronts. He lectured, sometimes with other fugitive slaves, including Ellen and William Craft. In 1849 the American Peace Society sent him to Paris, France, as a delegate to the Paris Peace Congress. While he was in Europe, the Fugitive Slave Law of 1850 was passed, which made it dangerous

*Antislavery picture from 1837*

for him to return to the United States. He remained in Europe for five years, delivering more than a thousand antislavery speeches and traveling more than 25,000 miles, a distance equivalent to circling the entire world. In 1854 a few English friends purchased his freedom from Enoch Price for $300, allowing him to return home.

It was said that, once he learned to read, William Wells Brown always carried a book in his pocket. Reading led to writing, and he became an author. His *Narrative of William Wells Brown, A Fugitive Slave* (1847) was a best-seller of its time. His other works include *Clotel; or, The President's Daughter* (1853), the first novel published by an African American, and *The Escape; or, A Leap for Freedom* (1858), the first play published by an African American. When she was only sixteen, his daughter Josephine Brown wrote *Biography of an American Bondman*, which provided much of the information about William Wells Brown for this chapter.

Despite his achievements and fame, William Wells Brown spent the rest of his life tormented by his inability to locate his mother, his sister, and the other members of his family. He died near Boston on November 6, 1884, at the age of seventy.

# CHAPTER EIGHT

# THE OBERLIN-WELLINGTON
# RESCUE OF JOHN PRICE

## *"They Can't Have Him!"*

*Major northern cities such as Philadelphia and Boston harbored many fugitive slaves, but a small town in northern Ohio became known as the nation's hotbed of abolitionism. With a population of only two thousand, Oberlin, Ohio, sheltered, at one time or another, a total of perhaps three thousand escaped slaves before the Civil War. In one famous incident, nearly the entire town came to the rescue of a fugitive slave.*

In 1833, John Shipherd and Philo Stewart, who had been childhood friends, founded the town and college of Oberlin, thirty-five miles southwest of Cleveland. The town and college attracted people who believed in the principle that all people are created equal. Oberlin College was the nation's first school of higher education to enroll female as well as male students, and one of the first to admit black students. Area residents elected a black Oberlin graduate, John Mercer Langston, as township clerk, making him the first black person elected to public office in the United States.

After slavery was outlawed in Canada in 1834, Oberlin became a popular stop for slaves fleeing northward. Six different Underground Railroad routes led to Oberlin. Of the three thousand fugitives who spent some time in Oberlin, several hundred decided to remain there to live. Even after the passage of the Fugitive Slave Law in 1850, many runaways lived openly in the town, for slave hunters were generally afraid to go there.

The Oberlin College faculty encouraged their students to travel about, preaching against slavery, during vacations and after graduation. There was a saying among abolitionists that wherever an Oberlin graduate settled, a new Underground Railroad station was begun. Some were so bold as to venture into the South, where they were shot at, beaten, and jailed for preaching abolitionism and helping slaves escape.

White southerners called Oberlin "nigger town" and hated it so intensely that they occasionally sent slave hunters there, despite the danger. When a fugitive couple was captured in Oberlin in 1841, students and townspeople chased the slave catchers to the nearby town of Elyria and helped the couple escape from jail. Another time, slave hunters followed a party of fugitives into Oberlin. A group of Oberlin students went to the building where the runaway slaves were hiding. The students painted their skin black and exchanged clothes with the fugitives, then drove off from the hiding place in a carriage at high speed. The slave hunters chased and caught the students; by the time they realized their mistake, the real fugitives were en route to Canada.

Many lawmakers—both southern and northern—wanted Oberlin punished for its defiance of the law. The town and college seemed to think that they were a nation unto themselves. Southern whites who came to inquire about their runaway slaves were not allowed to stay

*The image of a fugitive with his belongings tied to a stick became a famous antislavery symbol. This version dates from the early 1800s. Reportedly a road sign bearing a similar picture was put up outside Oberlin, Ohio, to point the way for fugitive slaves.*

at the college-owned Palmer House hotel in the center of town. The townspeople also refused to celebrate the Fourth of July, claiming there was no true independence as long as the country allowed slavery. Instead, Oberlinians celebrated Independence Day on August 1 —the anniversary of the date in 1834 when slavery became illegal in the British Empire. To proslavery people who argued that the Fugitive Slave Law was the national law and must be obeyed, Oberlinians said there was a Higher Law that proclaimed every person's right to be free.

By 1858, officials in President James Buchanan's administration were looking for a way to punish Oberlin, for they feared that the town's defiance would provoke a war with the South. The opportunity they were awaiting soon arose.

Two hundred miles south of Oberlin, in Kentucky's Mason County, lived two slaves named John and Dinah, who were cousins. John and Dinah belonged to John Bacon, whose farm lay just a quarter of a mile from the Ohio River. The cousins often spoke of escaping, for if they could somehow get across the river, they could travel north through Ohio, cross Lake Erie, and reach the free country of Canada. However, their owner usually watched them so carefully that they had no opportunity to escape.

During the cold winter of 1855–56 (the same winter in which Margaret Garner and her family crossed the Ohio), the river froze. In mid-January 1856, with the ice at its thickest, John Bacon and his wife and children went to visit relatives for several days. Bacon didn't suspect that his two slaves would run away. John had a deformed foot that made walking long distances difficult. Besides, Bacon had left a white man on the farm to watch the cousins.

After their master's departure, John and Dinah waited until dark and took two horses from the barn. Instead of riding directly to the river, they did something remarkably brave. Risking capture, they picked up a friend of theirs, Frank, who lived on a farm in the next county. With Dinah sharing a horse with one of the men, the three fugitives galloped to the river.

The Ohio was approximately a quarter-mile wide at the point where they crossed. Slipping and sliding on the ice, the fugitives managed to ride to the Ohio shore, but in the darkness they couldn't find a path leading up the riverbank. They searched through the night, their faces, fingers, and toes growing numb with the cold.

Finally, near sunrise, they could see well enough to locate a road leading onto the shore. They galloped up the path onto the snow-covered free soil of Ohio and continued on for several miles. Realizing that they would freeze to death if they didn't find shelter, they began to look for someone to help them.

Soon they encountered an elderly Quaker man, much as William Wells Brown had done. It wasn't by chance that Quakers often seemed almost magically to appear in these situations, for many of them chose to live in places frequented by fugitive slaves.

"Friends," said the elderly man, "thee must be nearly froze. Thee had better stop here in my house and warm."

The three fugitives were so stiff from the cold that the old man had to help them down from the horses. Not wanting to take anything from their master except themselves, John and Dinah then released the horses, which recrossed the river and were found by John Bacon a few days later. Meanwhile, the old man and his family cared for John, Dinah, and Frank in their home for two weeks. Around the first of February, the fugitives continued their journey on foot. For unknown reasons, Dinah separated from the two men and traveled on alone; she may have gone to Canada. Following the North Star, John and Frank gradually advanced northward.

Near Mansfield, Ohio, they were nearly caught. An abolitionist was giving them a ride to a UGRR station when his sleigh tipped over and John and Frank, hiding beneath a load of hay, tumbled out onto the snow. A politician who supported the Fugitive Slave Law happened to be passing and saw the runaway slaves. But instead of arresting them, he helped lift the sleigh out of the snowbank and sent them on their way. "For God's sake, don't ever tell anybody that I helped you," the politician begged the UGRR conductor.

Passed on from one UGRR station to another, John and Frank reached the home of a man who lived along Lake Erie near Toledo, Ohio. However, the same cold weather that had frozen the Ohio River had filled Lake Erie with ice chunks, hindering boat traffic. The two fugitives were advised to go to Oberlin, where they would surely be safe until the spring thaw permitted them to cross the lake into Canada.

One of the first things John did after arriving in Oberlin was adopt a last name: Price. He lodged with a black farmer outside town, and Frank settled nearby. John Price did farm work for a dollar a day. When he became ill, the townspeople came to his aid. John and Frank felt so welcome in Oberlin that they decided to remain there rather than go to Canada.

John and Frank lived peacefully in Oberlin for more than two years. Then, in the late summer of 1858, Anderson Jennings, a slave catcher from Kentucky, arrived in town. Jennings had been offered $500 each to capture and bring back John Price and Frank.

Carrying two revolvers and two sets of handcuffs in his pockets, Jennings checked into a flophouse called Wack's Hotel. Even around the "hotbed of abolitionism" there were some proslavery people, and Jennings recruited several of them to assist him. It was said that a ten-year-old boy passing Wack's Hotel noticed Jennings and his accomplices out on the porch and helped alert the townspeople to the presence of the "rough-looking" men.

Meanwhile, Jennings was preparing his trap. He visited Lewis Boynton, a farmer who sided with the southern slaveholders, at his house about two miles outside of town. Jennings offered the Boyntons' thirteen-year-old son, Shakespeare Boynton, $10 if he could lure John Price to come with him in a buggy, and another $10

Effects of the Fugitive Slave Law, *an 1850 lithograph showing fugitives being shot at by slave catchers*

if he could do the same with Frank. Young Shake Boynton agreed to help the slave catcher.

The next morning, Monday, September 13, 1858, Shake Boynton drove a horse and buggy to the farm where John Price was living. Shake told John that his father needed help digging potatoes and would pay John and Frank to do the job. John thanked the boy for thinking of them but said he had to take care of Frank, who had been injured a couple of nights earlier. However, he offered to introduce Shake to another friend who might need a job. Never dreaming that a thirteen-year-old boy would betray him, John offered to accompany Shake to find this other friend.

Shake said that he needed to stop at the blacksmith's but would soon return for Price. Instead of going to the blacksmith's, Shake went to Wack's Hotel to tell Jennings that he and Price would soon be passing along a certain road. Jennings knew that Oberlin citizens had been watching him, so rather than go himself, he dispatched three accomplices, including a fellow Kentucky slave hunter, to capture John Price.

When Shake Boynton returned, the unsuspecting Price climbed into his buggy. As they traveled along a dirt road, Price noticed a two-horse carriage with three men in it following behind them. Young Shake slowed his horse. Just as the buggy rolled to a stop, the carriage pulled up and two of its occupants leaped out and grabbed John Price. The Kentucky slave hunter pulled his gun and ordered John to get into their carriage.

Realizing that he was trapped, John said, "I'll go with you," and obeyed. The three men drove him toward Wellington, a town nine miles from Oberlin. A southbound train was due in Wellington at 5:13 that afternoon. John would be on that train in a few hours, and back in his master's hands in Kentucky in a day or two, his captors bragged.

As John was being taken to Wellington, Shake drove back to Jennings to collect his reward. Jennings was so pleased that he gave the boy the entire $20, even though Frank had not been captured. Jennings hired a buggy and headed to Wellington to meet his three comrades and John Price.

John pretended not to care that he was being returned to slavery, even asking the Kentuckian about events back home. But all along the road to Wellington, he looked for help, and he found it. He and his captors were passing a small cemetery when an Oberlin student named Ansel Lyman approached them on foot. Suddenly, John cried out for help. Seeing John with the three white men, the twenty-two-year-old student of English literature immediately figured out what had happened. Although he was a staunch abolitionist, Lyman knew he didn't stand a chance of rescuing the fugitive from three men who were probably armed, so he hurried into Oberlin for assistance.

The slave catchers arrived in Wellington with John Price in the early afternoon and checked into Wadsworth's Hotel. Jennings joined them around two-thirty. While awaiting the arrival of the 5:13 train, the four white men holed up with Price in an attic room, which Jennings considered a good position from which to fight off any abolitionists who might attempt a rescue.

As soon as he reached Oberlin, Ansel Lyman spread the alarm. Soon the whole town knew that slave hunters had seized John Price. Residents poured out of homes and stores. Professors halted classes so that they and their students could join the angry crowd. "They can't have him!" yelled the people gathering on the streets of the town.

Within minutes a cavalcade of carts, carriages, and wagons set out for Wellington. People who couldn't find room in a vehicle walked the nine miles. By about three o'clock an estimated five hundred people had surrounded Wadsworth's Hotel, and the crowd continued to grow. The protesters included whites and blacks, men and women, professors and students, grandparents and young children, shopkeepers, ministers, and politicians. Some of them waved guns as they shouted up to the top floor of the hotel: "Bring him out! Let Price go!"

Looking out the attic window, the slave hunters saw that they were vastly outnumbered. Still, they had several advantages. The fed-

*Wadsworth's Hotel; the semicircular window at top looks out from the attic room where John Price was held.*

eral Fugitive Slave Law was on their side. Also, the crowd was so large that no one seemed to be in charge, with the result that people stood around, making threats without actually doing anything. In addition, the slave hunters had wired to the city of Cleveland for help. If Jennings and his men could delay long enough, hundreds of soldiers might arrive to assist them.

To kill time, Jennings went out onto the hotel balcony and addressed the crowd. "I want no trouble with the people of Ohio," he declared. "This boy is mine by the laws of Kentucky and the United States!"

"There are no slaves in Ohio and never will be!" someone in the crowd yelled back at him.

"But the boy is willing to return to Kentucky," Jennings protested.

"Let him come out and speak!" came the response.

Jennings told John Price to go out onto the balcony and say that he didn't mind returning to John Bacon's farm. With guns aimed at him from behind, he had no choice but to obey. "I suppose I've got to go back to Kentucky," he said, but the crowd saw that he didn't mean it.

The 5:13 train arrived at the Wellington station, waited a few minutes, and then chugged on without John Price. The situation at the hotel remained a stalemate. The heavily armed slave catchers continued to hold Price, while the crowd outside was undecided about what to do. A rumor spread through the crowd that the next train, scheduled to arrive at eight, would contain troops sent to enforce the Fugitive Slave Law. If Price wasn't rescued by then, he might be returned to slavery.

Near sunset two small groups decided to attempt a rescue. One was led by William Lincoln, who was studying to become a minister. Heading toward the hotel's front entrance, Lincoln was followed by five men, including his classmate Ansel Lyman. The other group was led by John Scott, a black man who owned a harness store in Oberlin. Five or six men followed Scott to the hotel's back door.

The slave catchers had posted guards at both entrances. Those at the front door tried to push William Lincoln and his men away. A fistfight erupted, which Lincoln ended by aiming his revolver at the head of a guard. "Quit, or I'll blow your brains out!" he threatened.

As the guards retreated to a side room, Lincoln yelled, "Forward! Forward!" and charged up the stairway toward the attic where John Price was being held.

Meanwhile, Scott and his men broke through the back door and confronted several other guards. One of Scott's men was so enraged over the kidnapping that he threatened, "The first man who keeps us from going upstairs I will shoot." Seconds later, he aimed his gun at a guard standing in the way and pulled the trigger. At the last moment, Scott pushed the gun barrel and the bullet struck the ceiling instead of killing anyone. The shot scared off the guards, clearing the way to the stairs.

The two groups of rescuers met in the hallway outside the attic. It was so dark that neither the slave catchers nor the rescuers were sure what was happening. Three Oberlin College students made the final rescue. William Lincoln and a classmate forced the door open. Richard Winsor, an Oberlin student who was Price's Sunday school teacher, grabbed the fugitive and took him down the stairs. Winsor and Price climbed into a buggy and raced off to Oberlin.

Anderson Jennings and his men did not try to pursue Price, for their goal now was to save their own lives. But, having achieved what they wanted, the crowd did nothing further to threaten the kidnappers. As the buggy carrying John Price disappeared in the distance, the onlookers cheered and threw their hats high into the air in triumph. The crowd then gradually thinned out as people began to head home.

There was still a chance that troops would be sent to recapture John, so he had to be hidden once he reached Oberlin. Several of the Rescuers (as people who took part in freeing Price became known) discussed the situation. For a short while a bookstore owner hid John in a secret room in his home. However, since he was a known UGRR conductor, his house was likely to be searched if federal officials came looking for Price.

It was decided that Professor James Fairchild's home was safer. A minister and a professor of mathematics and science at Oberlin College, Fairchild was not known to have ever harbored runaway slaves. Moreover, he was not linked to the Rescuers because he and his family had been away visiting friends in a nearby town all day.

James and Mary Fairchild welcomed John into their home, taking him up to a rear room on the second floor. The couple then gathered their six children and told them the story of the fugitive's capture and rescue. "You must never tell anyone in the world that John is here," whispered Mrs. Fairchild, "or your father could be arrested and

*Professor James Fairchild's home in Oberlin, where John Price was hidden in a second-floor room*

*Plaque in Oberlin's Martin Luther King Park honoring the jailed Rescuers*

jailed." She explained that they were doing good by defying an evil law.

John remained with the Fairchilds for a few days and then was taken to Canada. The Rescuers did such a fine job of keeping his trip to Canada secret that, to this day, no one knows where he settled or what became of him. The Fairchild children also kept silent. Neither the slave hunters nor the federal government learned of their father's involvement in the case. Even eight years later, when James Fairchild was named president of Oberlin College, few people knew that he had once hidden John Price in his home on Professor Street.

The Oberlin-Wellington Rescue became famous around the country. To abolitionists, the episode was a triumph of good over evil, a victory for the Higher Law over politicians' compromises. They pointed out that the Rescuers had shown themselves to be peaceful, for they had not shed any blood, despite greatly outnumbering the kidnappers. As southern slaveholders saw it, on the other hand, the Ohioans had broken the law of the United States and must be punished. Unfortunately, the U.S. government agreed with the South. President Buchanan and his advisers figured they could accomplish two goals by prosecuting the Rescuers: punish Oberlin for hiding so many fugitives in the past, and show the South that the federal government would enforce the Fugitive Slave Law.

The U.S. government charged thirty-seven people—twenty-five from Oberlin and twelve from the Wellington area —with helping John Price escape. Those charged included an Oberlin College professor, Henry Peck; Ohio state legislator Ralph Plumb; schoolteacher Charles Langston (brother of John Mercer Langston, the country's first elected African American official); a physician; two lawyers; a minister; two Sunday school teachers; and the mayor of Wellington, Loring Wadsworth. The oldest of the accused was seventy-four-year-old Matthew Gillet, a farmer and UGRR conductor. The youngest were several Oberlin College students in their twenties, including William Lincoln, Ansel Lyman, and Richard Winsor. Except for a man who had been fined $1 for smoking a cigar on the streets of Oberlin, the defendants had virtually spotless records, yet they were arrested and placed in jail in Cleveland.

William Lincoln was teaching school in Dublin, Ohio, when he was arrested. A constable and a deputy sheriff burst into the schoolhouse and held Lincoln at gunpoint in front of his class. As he hand-

even rumored that Ohio state troops would go to war with the federal government over the case. Had that happened, the Civil War might have begun in Ohio in 1859 instead of in South Carolina in 1861.

During the trial, the U.S. government hoped that the Rescuers would admit they had been wrong to break the Fugitive Slave Law. Instead, they became more determined than ever to defy it. One Rescuer wrote from jail: "When I am out again, I will rescue the first slave I get a chance to rescue." The schoolteacher Charles Langston made a defiant speech in front of the judge: "So help me God!" he said, "I stand here to say that I will do all I can, for any man thus seized and held [like John Price], though the penalty of six months imprisonment for each offense hangs over me. We have a common humanity. *You* would [help a fugitive slave]. Your friends would honor you for doing it. Your children would honor you for doing it. And every good and honest man would say you had done *right!*" Langston's speech sparked such loud applause that the judge threatened to clear the courtroom if another outburst like it occurred.

The U.S. government realized that its plan had backfired, and that by prosecuting the Rescuers it had just created more antislavery sentiment in the North. Southerners were outraged that the men who had come looking for escaped slaves had been jailed, as though they were the ones who had broken the law. Anderson Jennings and his fellow slave catchers were so eager to return home that they agreed to drop the proceedings and signed a paper promising "never again to hunt fugitives in northern Ohio." Then, at five o'clock on the afternoon of July 6, 1859, the Rescuers were released after about three months in prison.

Outside the prison, hundreds of people gathered to greet them.

As a band played "Yankee Doodle" and a hundred cannons fired a salute from the lakefront, the Rescuers marched with their supporters to the Cleveland train station.

When their train pulled into Oberlin at sunset, the Rescuers were greeted by three thousand people, more than lived in the entire town. Wherever he was in Canada, John Price would have been proud if he could have seen what the people of Oberlin did on the night of the Rescuers' return. They held a gigantic rally, at which they pledged that "no fugitive slave shall ever be taken from Oberlin if we have power to prevent it."

# CHAPTER NINE

# JOHN ANDERSON
### *"No Man Should Take Me Alive!"*

*With thousands of American slaves fleeing to Canada, black communities were established in many Canadian cities and towns, including Toronto, St. Catharines, Chatham, and Windsor. Black Canadians, who numbered approximately 25,000 by 1860, voted, paid taxes, served on juries, and generally enjoyed the same rights as other Canadian citizens.*

*Occasionally, however, American slave hunters violated British law and crossed the Canadian border to pursue fugitives. Also, now and then the United States asked its neighbor to the north to return escaped slaves. John Anderson, a fugitive who settled in Canada, faced both of these threats to his freedom. For a short period the international tug-of-war over Anderson threatened to ignite a real war between the United States and Canada.*

Born around 1831, John Anderson belonged to Moses Burton, a tobacco farmer in Howard County, Missouri. Rebelliousness ran in John's family. Soon after John's birth his father ran away. He report-

130

*John Anderson*

edly fooled Mr. Burton by heading south instead of north, and eventually sailed to South America. When John was about seven, Mrs. Burton tried to whip his mother, who fought back, pulling a clump of hair from her mistress's head. John's mother was immediately sent down the Mississippi River and sold to a Louisiana planter. The young slave boy never saw either of his parents again.

John was raised by Mr. and Mrs. Burton, who bragged that "Jackey," as they called him, was "almost like a member of the family." Mrs. Burton had him call her Mother, and for a few years kept him around the house as a playmate for the Burtons' two daughters. At the age of fourteen or fifteen, John was sent out to work in the tobacco fields. Moses Burton taught him about tobacco growing, and, while John was still a teenager, made him supervisor of the Burtons' other field slaves. The Burtons rewarded John's diligence by giving him a patch of land on which to grow a little tobacco of his own.

Around the age of nineteen, John fell in love with a young slave woman from a neighboring farm. Maria Tomlin came from an unusual background. Her father, a barber in the nearby town of Fayette, Missouri, had saved enough money to buy himself and Maria's mother out of slavery. But to buy his daughter would cost about $1,000, and he was having difficulty saving that much. So Maria remained a slave even though her parents were free.

John visited Maria on her owner's farm several times. Mr. Tomlin was angry about this, for he still hoped to save enough money to free his daughter, while John seemed likely to remain a slave forever. But Maria and John loved each other despite her father's objections. Realizing that he could eventually buy his daughter's freedom but not her heart, Lewis Tomlin relented, and the young couple had a slave wedding.

Mr. Burton permitted John to visit his wife on weekends. Each Friday night, John walked to Maria's cabin on the nearby farm, returning to the Burtons' before dawn on Monday. After a year or two of marriage, the couple had a child. The new father dreamed of one day buying his family's freedom, but since he earned just a few dollars a year from his tobacco patch, that seemed highly unlikely.

Being with his wife and child made John so happy that he began spending more time with them. Besides weekends, he sometimes walked there late on weeknights, rushing back to the Burtons' before daybreak. Mr. Burton was annoyed that John came and went without asking permission. He was also displeased that John had married a woman from another plantation. Had John married one of the Burton slave women, Mr. Burton would have owned the baby.

Suddenly, John wasn't almost like a member of the family anymore, especially since Mrs. Burton, who had been partial to him, had died. Early one morning as John returned from visiting Maria and their baby, Mr. Burton confronted him. "Jackey, where have you been?" he demanded.

"Oh, I've been walking about," said John, realizing that Burton knew where he had been.

"I'll walk *you* about!" said Mr. Burton, enraged by this smart-alecky answer. He took out his whip and tried to beat John. Showing his mother's spirit, John refused to be beaten. He may have even pulled the whip out of his master's hands. Burton then fetched his gun from the house and threatened to shoot John if he didn't submit to a whipping. John continued to stare at him defiantly. Fortunately Burton's daughters overheard the commotion and convinced him to put down his gun.

His fury cooling, Burton claimed that he had only meant to frighten John, not actually shoot him. "But I will sell you to someone who will break your spirit!" he vowed.

Soon afterward, in August 1853, Burton sold John to Colonel Reuben McDaniel of Saline County, Missouri, for $1,000. During the buggy ride to McDaniel's plantation, which was located twenty-five miles or more from Maria and his child, John's new owner warned him about trying to escape: "If you attempt to flee, I will give you a good flogging and sell you down to New Orleans!"

John was put to work in the colonel's fields. The separation from

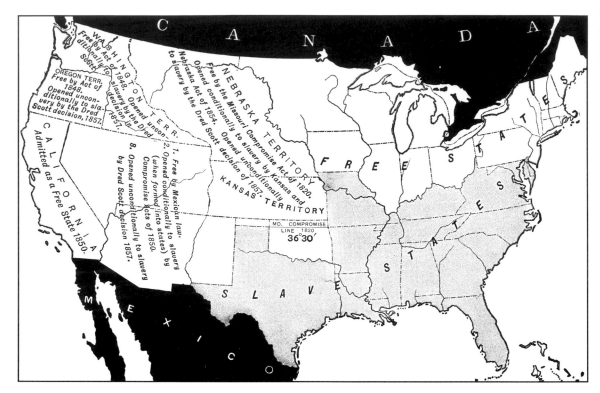

*Map showing the slave states (gray) and free states (white) as of 1857. Canada did not allow slavery.*

his wife and child threw him into despair. After a few weeks he pleaded with McDaniel to allow him to visit his family. John would never see them again, the colonel answered, so he might as well choose a slave woman on his plantation for a new wife. Hearing that, John resolved to run away and rescue his family.

John had heard an elderly slave speak of Canada, a place far to the north where everyone was free. One Sunday in late September of 1853, Colonel McDaniel attended a meeting at his church to discuss the case of a neighbor who had whipped a slave to death. Seeing his opportunity, John took a mule and rode back toward his wife and child.

It took him all day to reach Fayette. First he visited his father-in-law, who had become very fond of him. Mr. Tomlin agreed that John should flee northward, perhaps to Canada, and offered him a pistol to use against slave hunters, if the need arose. John refused the gun, saying that he had a knife with which to defend himself. He then visited the slave cabin where he had spent so many happy hours.

He kissed Maria and their child and said that he would do everything he could to free them once he reached Canada. It was too dangerous for him to remain with his family overnight, so at around midnight he set out, his face toward the North Star. He later recalled that, as he departed on his journey, "I made up my mind that no man should take me alive!"

John Anderson seems to have spent most of the next day hiding, in case Colonel McDaniel pursued him. Seeing no evidence that he was being hunted, on Tuesday he set out in broad daylight. At midday he was walking past a farm when he crossed paths with a white man named Seneca Digges, his eight-year-old son, Ben, and four of their slaves. Suspicious of Anderson, Digges demanded to see his pass. John had none, but claimed that he had his master's permission to be away from home.

Under Missouri law, a white man was expected to stop any suspicious-looking black person and was eligible for a $5 reward if that person proved to be a runaway slave. Convinced that the stranger's story was a lie, Digges ordered John to come along to his farm and join his slaves at their noon meal. John knew that once they reached Digges's home, the white man would pull out a gun and arrest him. He went along for a way, then suddenly broke loose and dashed into the woods.

Digges ordered his slaves to help him catch John. Everyone involved later told a different version of what occurred. Apparently,

Digges and his slaves armed themselves with clubs and encircled the runaway. "If you come near me, I will kill you!" John warned, pulling out his knife. Seneca Digges threw an ax at John, who dodged it and ran past his attackers, heading for a fence. He was starting to climb it when Digges attempted to grab him. Desperate to avoid capture, John stabbed Digges and saw the blood spurt out of him, but he didn't stop. As little Ben Digges bent over his wounded father, John scrambled over the fence and got away.

Had he been captured before he met Digges, Anderson would have been returned to Colonel McDaniel, who might have whipped him and sold him down to New Orleans. Now that he had stabbed a white man, he was likely to be hanged without a trial. John did something remarkable for a man facing death if caught: He retraced his steps and returned to his wife's cabin. He thought he had little chance to escape, and he wanted to see his family one last time. After he told Maria what had occurred, the couple said a last farewell and John slipped off into the darkness.

He had learned a lesson about being seen in the daytime, and now he traveled only at night. He walked across the state of Missouri to the Mississippi River, where he found a boat and crossed into Illinois. Although now in a free state, he knew that he must reach Canada, for Missouri slaveholders would pursue him anywhere within the borders of the United States.

Following his skirmish with John Anderson, Seneca Digges had been carried to a doctor's house. He lingered for thirteen days before dying of his wounds. As Anderson walked north through Illinois, a small army of slave hunters pursued him, seeking the $1,000 reward offered for his capture.

The UGRR helped John Anderson on his journey. One night, an

English settler fed and sheltered him. At another farmhouse he received a loaf of bread. After a few weeks, he arrived in Chicago. From there, abolitionists sent him via the UGRR to Detroit, Michigan. He crossed the Detroit River and entered Windsor, Canada, in November 1853, after a two-month, seven-hundred-mile journey. At last he believed he was safe, because any slave catcher who pursued him would be breaking the laws of Canada and the British Empire.

As Canada's southernmost city, Windsor was a popular refuge for escaped slaves from the United States. For a few weeks Anderson worked for a Canadian railroad. He rented a room in a boardinghouse and attended a school for ex-slaves. But freedom without his wife and child left him a sad man. One day a teacher at the school, Laura Haviland, asked him what was wrong. He poured his heart out to her, telling her how he yearned for his family in Missouri. Haviland, who had helped a number of slaves escape on the UGRR while living in Michigan and Ohio, decided to help reunite John with his loved ones.

Mrs. Haviland wrote to John Anderson's father-in-law to see if his daughter and grandchild could be smuggled out of Missouri. She did not mail her letter from Windsor, for if it was intercepted, the postmark would reveal John's whereabouts. She returned to her home near Adrian, Michigan, about fifty miles southwest of the Canadian border, and mailed the letter from there.

In the spring of 1854, a letter allegedly from Mr. Tomlin arrived for Mrs. Haviland in Adrian. Mr. Tomlin claimed to have worked out a plan. He would pretend that Maria was his free wife rather than his slave daughter and would take her and her child out of Missouri to be with John. Mrs. Haviland sent a message to John Anderson in Canada informing him of the good news, but warning him not to get too excited until she found out more about the scheme.

*Escaped slaves who settled in Windsor, Canada*

A few days later, two men visited Mrs. Haviland at her Michigan home. The strangers, one of whom had a southern accent, claimed to be Underground Railroad conductors who had led John Anderson's family to Detroit. If Mrs. Haviland would tell John to go to a certain place in Detroit, said the two men, he would be reunited with his family.

Mrs. Haviland did not believe the two strangers' story. As soon as they departed, she sent John Anderson a telegram. He must leave Windsor immediately and go farther into Canada, she warned, for she suspected that the two men were actually slave catchers.

Mrs. Haviland had figured correctly. The two men were a Missouri slave hunter named Brown and a detective who was assisting him. The letter signed "Lewis Tomlin" was a fake. In fact, for briefly sheltering his son-in-law, Mr. Tomlin had been arrested, whipped, and driven out of Missouri. Maria and her child were being watched so closely they couldn't possibly escape. Missouri law officers had intercepted Mrs. Haviland's letter to Tomlin and had forged the response, trying to lure John Anderson to Detroit. If Anderson crossed the border, instead of meeting his wife and child he would be seized by Brown and several detectives.

John Anderson was crestfallen when Mrs. Haviland's telegram was read to him and he learned what had happened. But he followed her advice and moved on to Chatham, a town with a large number of fugitive slaves fifty miles farther from the U.S. border. He changed his name, too, hoping to confuse anyone who pursued him.

Soon after his arrival in Chatham, there was a disturbing incident. Brown and his associates arrived in town and began asking about a black man from Missouri called Jackey or John Anderson. Recognizing Brown as a slave hunter, a group of black Chatham residents surrounded him and threatened to hang him from the nearest tree. Brown pulled his gun and held off the angry crowd until the Chatham police arrived to rescue him and his comrades. Canadian authorities made no attempt to arrest the people who had threatened Brown's life. Most Canadians considered it shameful that the United States allowed slavery and felt that anyone who pursued runaway slaves into their country was not worthy of mercy.

No longer safe in Chatham, John Anderson traveled farther into the interior of Canada. He moved from town to town, working as a bricklayer and plasterer. Brown and the other slave catchers finally gave up their hunt, and in 1858, when Anderson had been in Canada five years, he settled down, buying a house in the town of Caledonia, near Brantford. He lived there two years, a hardworking and respected member of the community, but inwardly heartbroken about the family he had left in the States.

One day in the spring of 1860, as John Anderson collected sap from his trees in preparation for making maple syrup, a sheriff suddenly appeared. He reluctantly told John that he had a warrant for his arrest. On what charge, Anderson wanted to know. The murder of a man in Missouri seven years ago, said the sheriff.

Anderson was locked in the Brantford jail. He learned that Missouri officials, including the governor and secretary of state, had filed papers requesting that Canada return him if he were ever located. They claimed that Canada's antislavery laws did not protect Anderson because he had committed murder and must be tried for the crime. A neighbor, to whom John had confided his life story, had informed on him.

In jail, Anderson said that he hadn't known until his arrest that Seneca Digges had died. However, he insisted that he had "always felt that I had a right to my freedom" and explained that he wouldn't have stabbed Digges had he not attempted to deprive him of his liberty.

Anderson's arrest outraged most Canadians, including government officials and newspaper editors. They pointed out that, during his years in Canada, Anderson had proved himself to be a peaceful, law-abiding man. Stabbing Seneca Digges had been an act of self-defense, for Digges had tried to seize him and return him to slavery. Far from viewing Anderson as a criminal, many Canadians called him a hero, who had waged his own small war against an evil institution.

John Anderson would have been released had the Canadian public been allowed to decide his fate, but the case was not theirs to settle. Instead, the legal and political issues sparked an international feud among the United States, Canada, and England.

In 1842, the United States and Great Britain had signed the Webster-Ashburton Treaty, which resolved several disputes between the United States and Canada. One article of the treaty provided that people wanted for murder and other serious crimes could not escape punishment by fleeing across the border between the two nations. The United States and Canada agreed to extradite people wanted for serious crimes in each other's countries.

The question was: Did the article apply to a fugitive slave who had killed someone while escaping? American abolitionists and most Canadians said no, killing a person who stood in the way of one's freedom was not murder. The Englishman Lord Ashburton had once told the American abolitionist Lewis Tappan that the treaty hadn't been intended to include acts committed by escaping slaves as extra-ditable crimes. Ashburton's opinion meant a great deal, for he and Daniel Webster of the United States had *made* the Webster-Ashburton Treaty.

But in the southern United States, white planters and politicians claimed that what Lord Ashburton or Daniel Webster had intended didn't matter. The treaty said that accused murderers must be returned, so John Anderson must be sent back to Missouri.

James Buchanan, the president of the United States from 1857 to 1861, could have used his influence to free John Anderson. However, Buchanan maintained the position he had held regarding the Oberlin-Wellington Rescue trial of the previous year. Afraid that the southern states might secede if the federal government interfered with slavery, Buchanan wanted Anderson delivered to Missouri. On October 2, 1860, the U.S. Department of State formally asked that Canada return John Anderson to Missouri. The full weight of the U.S. government was now pressuring Canada to hand over the fugitive to

the country's newspapers deriding the decision as "un-British" and "too narrowly technical," English officials refused to allow the Canadian ruling to stand. On January 9, 1861, they ordered the governor of Canada not to return John Anderson to Missouri; a few days later they ruled that Anderson must be sent to England for the courts there to decide his case.

Canadians were torn. They hoped that England would free Anderson, yet resented the Mother Country for overruling their courts. At this period in history, many Canadians favored independence from England, which the United States had achieved almost eighty years earlier. The Mother Country's disregard for their courts intensified anti-British sentiment among Canadians. Some who favored independence even spoke of joining with the northern United States to form a new slavery-free nation.

While the United States, Canada, and England argued over him, John Anderson sat in the Toronto jail. Canadian officials did not send him to England, for they were eager to hold his appeal trial, both to free him and to demonstrate that they would decide their own affairs. In the United States, the situation was changing rapidly. Abraham Lincoln had been elected president on November 6, 1860. Believing that President Lincoln would end slavery, the southern states had begun withdrawing from the Union on December 20, just five days after the verdict in Toronto. With a civil war over slavery looming, there was no longer a reason to appease southern slaveholders, so the U.S. government eased its pressure on Canada to return Anderson.

Anderson's appeal was held in Toronto in February 1861. Ultimately, the case was not settled according to any ideals about freedom and justice. It was decided on a single word. The appeals court judges ruled that John Anderson should be freed because the original warrant for his arrest had charged him with "killing" rather than "murdering" Seneca Digges. Killing wasn't necessarily a crime, for it could include an accident or an act of self-defense. Because of that one word, John Anderson was free to go.

As a crowd congratulated him, Anderson stood up and told the judges: "Thank you, gentlemen. Thank you, your lordships." Anderson's friends and supporters called for a sleigh and took him around the snow-covered city at the head of a parade, celebrating his triumph.

But abolitionists in the United States, Canada, and England were disappointed. True, John Anderson was free, but instead of condemning slavery, the judges had merely condemned the wording of the warrant. Since it was possible that a new, properly worded warrant would be issued, Anderson would have to leave Canada. While plans were being made about where he would settle, Anderson gave a speech before a large crowd at a Toronto church. He asked that he be remembered as neither a murderer nor a hero, but simply as a man who had wanted to free his family and himself. Soon afterward, abolitionists in England invited him to their country. In the spring of 1861, he left for England by steamship.

Anderson was amazed by all the attention he received in England. In London, the John Anderson Committee was created to help him raise money to free his wife and child. At one enormous gathering, Anderson spoke before more than six thousand people about his life in slavery, his escape, and his dream of locating and liberating his family.

Over the next few months, Anderson traveled around England making similar speeches. He also related his experiences to an English abolitionist, Harper Twelvetrees, with whom he produced a book titled *The Story of the Life of John Anderson, The Fugitive Slave.*

On April 12, 1861—about the time that John Anderson had left for England—the U.S. Civil War began. John learned some distressing news: Maria's owner had been killed near the beginning of the war and all of his slaves had been sold. Maria and their child might be anywhere in the slave states.

After Anderson finished his lecture tour, his abolitionist friends decided that he should attend school in a small English town. He had little choice, for he was so despised by southerners that they might seize him if he returned to the United States or Canada. For a year he attended school in Corby, England.

His English friends then decided to send him to Africa to live. He was offered free passage and a grant of land in Liberia, an African country that had been founded by freed slaves in 1822. He apparently didn't want to live in Liberia, for it was thousands of miles from his family, but he reluctantly agreed to go.

On December 24, 1862, John Anderson was placed aboard a steamship bound for Liberia. Whether he arrived is unknown. There is no evidence that he ever lived in Liberia, and a man from Missouri later claimed to have met him in a European port. Did he jump ship, live in Europe for a few years, and then return to the United States after the northern victory in the Civil War freed all the remaining slaves in 1865? Did he spend the rest of his life searching for Maria and their child, and perhaps even find them? It seems possible that he did return to America to look for his family, for he wasn't a man who gave up easily. But exactly what became of him after he boarded the steamer on Christmas Eve, 1862, remains a mystery.

# CHAPTER TEN

# ANN MARIA WEEMS

## "My Child, Is It Really You?"

*M*ost *fugitive slaves were adults between the ages of about twenty-five and fifty. Now and then, elderly people fled slavery, but they were generally taken along by their sons and daughters. Sometimes, very young people escaped, but they usually accompanied their parents. A fifteen-year-old Maryland girl was one of the youngest slaves to flee without a parent as a guide.*

Ann Maria Weems was a house slave belonging to Charles Price, a slave trader who lived on a farm about fifteen miles from Washington, D.C., around Rockville, Maryland. Ann Maria waited on Mr. Price and his wife, serving them meals and cleaning house.

Mr. Price sometimes raped his female slaves, especially when he was drunk. Ann Maria wondered why Mrs. Price often whipped one particular slave boy for no apparent reason. She later learned that Mrs. Price resented the boy because he was the son of her husband and a slave woman. By the age of thirteen, Ann Maria was thinking about escaping, for she was terrified that her master would soon rape her, too.

Various slaveholders in the area owned many of Ann Maria's

*Ann Maria Weems posing as Joe Wright,*
*a young male carriage driver*

relatives. J. Bigelow, an abolitionist lawyer in Washington, D.C., became interested in freeing Ann Maria and her family. He raised $1,000 to buy Ann Maria's mother out of slavery and $1,600 to liberate one of Ann Maria's sisters. Once free, Mrs. Weems raised $1,100 to release her son Augustus, who had been sold down to Alabama. But when Bigelow asked Mr. Price about Ann Maria, he wouldn't sell her.

For two years Price refused Bigelow's offers to purchase Ann Maria's freedom. Finally, the lawyer realized that nothing would induce the slave dealer to part with the girl, and that she would have to escape via the UGRR. Her mother and other relatives had settled in Washington, D.C., but that city was too near the Price plantation for Ann Maria to live there without danger. Not even Boston would be safe, for Mr. Price might pursue her there. Ann Maria Weems would have to go to Canada, beyond the reach of the Fugitive Slave Law. Bigelow hoped to send her to Dresden, where her aunt and uncle had settled after fleeing on the UGRR.

By the time Ann Maria was fifteen, Mr. Price suspected she might try to escape. He made her sleep on the floor of his and his wife's bedroom so that she couldn't run off at night. Price's suspicions were well founded, for just then Bigelow was writing letters to William Still in Philadelphia about Ann Maria's impending dash for freedom. Because helping a slave escape was a serious crime in the United States, the lawyer did not sign his letters "J. Bigelow" or use the actual names of people involved in the plot. He signed his letters "William Penn," in honor of the Quaker founder of Pennsylvania, who had believed in the equality of all people.

In October 1855, Ann Maria Weems escaped from Mr. and Mrs. Price. How she did it is not known. Two of her cousins—a young man of about twenty-three and a young woman of about eighteen—may have helped her slip away. Ann Maria went to Washington, D.C., perhaps visiting her family briefly before continuing on to Bigelow's home.

Mr. Price offered $500 for the capture and return of his fugitive slave. Seeking the reward, slave hunters prowled the nation's capital searching for Ann Maria. Bigelow was unable to transport her out of the city—or even out of his home—for six weeks.

During that time, Bigelow and William Still concocted a plan. Still convinced his family physician, a Philadelphia medical professor he

really *was* talking to a young man. "The doctor went expressly to Washington after a young girl, who was to be brought away dressed up as a boy, and I took you to be the person," he said.

Ann Maria rose and walked out of the house. Still followed and learned the truth when they were beyond the hearing of everyone else. She had kept her word to Dr. H. and would reveal her identity only when alone with the famous UGRR leader.

Ann Maria enjoyed Thanksgiving dinner with the Still family. During the next two or three days, while Ann Maria stayed in his home, William Still made arrangements to send her farther north. Then, again dressed as a boy, she was sent along the UGRR to New York, to the home of Lewis Tappan, a prominent merchant and abolitionist who lived in Brooklyn.

Tappan, who was nearly seventy years old, had given so much money and aid to the cause that he was considered a UGRR "stock-

*Neck chain and leg shackles that once bound American slaves*

holder." With his brother Arthur Tappan, Lewis had founded the American and Foreign Anti-Slavery Society in 1840. In those days there was no national Thanksgiving and states held the holiday at various times, so Ann Maria had a second Thanksgiving feast while being sheltered in the Tappan home. His grandchildren asked why he was sending turkey and plum pudding upstairs, but Lewis Tappan didn't tell them that the food was for a fugitive slave.

While Ann Maria spent a day or two in his house, Lewis Tappan arranged for Reverend A. N. Freeman, a black minister from Brooklyn, to accompany her the rest of the way to her aunt and uncle in Dresden. Reverend Freeman and Joe Wright boarded a train in New York City. They carefully observed the other passengers on the trip across New York State, for, as Reverend Freeman later wrote: "Knowing that there was a large reward offered for Joe's apprehension, I feared there might be some lurking spy ready to pounce upon us."

To reach Canada, the train had to cross over Suspension Bridge near Niagara Falls. Reverend Freeman believed that this was the most dangerous part of their journey, for slave catchers might be waiting to seize them just before they entered Canada. The moment they reached the Canadian side of the falls, Reverend Freeman cried, "Thank God, we are safe in Canada!" But Ann Maria's joy was mingled with worry. If they couldn't find her aunt and uncle, she would be alone in a country where she didn't know a soul.

On a cold winter night in December 1855, their train arrived in Chatham, where Eliza Harris had settled and where John Anderson had briefly lived. It was now about two months since Ann Maria had fled from her master and mistress in Maryland, four hundred miles to the southeast. The roads were so muddy that Ann Maria and Reverend Freeman had to remain in Chatham two nights. On Monday morning, they found a driver who would take them in a wagon the twenty miles to Dresden.

They were making their way slowly along the slippery road when they came upon two black men, one on foot and the other on horseback. Reverend Freeman asked them if they knew the way to the home of Mr. and Mrs. Bradley, Ann Maria's uncle and aunt.

The man on horseback said it was about a mile farther, adding, "I reckon I am the one you want to find. My name is Bradley."

Just then Ann Maria turned her head to look at him. As soon as her uncle saw her face, he recognized her, even though she was still dressed as a boy. "My Lord, Maria, is that you? My child, is it really you?" her uncle said. "We never expected to see you again! We had given you up! Oh, what will your aunt say?"

As they approached his house, he yelled out, "Ann Maria's coming yonder!"

Ann Maria's aunt rushed up to the gate. Tears streaming from her eyes, she cried, "Ann Maria, is it you?" The fifteen-year-old girl leaped down from the wagon and began kissing and hugging her aunt as they both wept for joy. Then they all went into the house, where Ann Maria talked to her aunt and uncle late into the night. Every now and then, Ann Maria's aunt would suddenly burst into tears and say, "My child, you are here! Thank God, you are free!"

"Such a scene I never before witnessed," Reverend Freeman wrote in a letter to Lewis Tappan. Reverend Freeman ate dinner with the family and then began the long return trip home to Brooklyn.

Ann Maria Weems remained in Canada with her aunt and uncle, who sent her to school in a nearby community. The last that was known about her, she was awaiting the arrival of her mother and other relatives from Washington, D.C.

# CHAPTER ELEVEN

# SOLOMON NORTHUP

## *Nobody Knew His Name*

*A*n eighth of all African Americans of the early and mid-1800s were free. They included some who had purchased their liberty, some who had been freed by the terms of their owner's will, and some whose ancestors had escaped slavery or come to America voluntarily. But even free blacks faced dangers and hardships unknown to white citizens. Chief among them was the possibility of being kidnapped and sold south into slavery.

Easy money lured people into man-stealing, as it was called. A typical slave was worth $1,000, while those with special skills sold for $1,500 or even $2,000. At a time when the average worker earned about $500 a year, a man could become rich by kidnapping and selling a few people. Sadly, laws and customs also encouraged man-stealing. In the South, all black people without free papers were assumed to be slaves. Throughout the country, authorities almost always accepted a white person's word over an African American's. The

*Fugitive Slave Law of 1850 also endangered free blacks. According to this law, federal commissioners were to rule whether a person seized by slave hunters was a free black or a slave. A commissioner was paid $5 if he ruled that the black person was free, but $10 if he decided that the person was a slaveholder's property. The larger fee encouraged commissioners to decide in favor of the slave catchers—regardless of the facts in the case.*

*Kidnapped blacks were generally sent far from home to the Deep South, where their loved ones couldn't find them. Their names were changed, making them more difficult to find. Since slaves weren't allowed to write letters or testify in court, they had little chance to reveal their whereabouts or win their release from bondage, as a man named Solomon Northup tragically discovered.*

Solomon Northup was born in 1808 in Minerva, a small town in upstate New York not far from Canada. New York allowed slavery until 1827, when Solomon was nineteen years old. Solomon was born free, however, because his mother was free. Solomon's father was an ex-slave who had been freed around 1800 by the will of his owner, a wealthy man named Northup.

Solomon was a studious boy. When not helping his parents on the family farm, he read books or played his violin. He became so fine a fiddler that neighbors hired him to perform at parties and dances.

On Christmas Day, 1829, Solomon married a neighbor named Anne Hampton. The couple settled in Saratoga Springs, New York, a popular vacation resort not far from Albany, the state capital.

*Solomon Northup as a slave*

During the tourist season, Solomon and Anne worked at hotels in town. At other times, Solomon earned money by driving a carriage, playing his violin, and doing construction work, while Anne traveled twenty miles to the town of Hudson Falls to work as head cook at Sherrill's Coffee House. The couple had three children and were considered hardworking and devoted parents by everyone who knew them. They had many white as well as black friends, including Henry B. Northup, a lawyer related to the man who had owned Solomon's father.

The next day the three men watched the funeral procession along with thousands of other people. Afterward, Brown and Hamilton invited Solomon to join them for a few drinks at a tavern. Upon his return to the hotel, Solomon's head began to ache and he felt nauseated. He lay down in his room and fell into a delirium, for his two "friends" had drugged his drinks. During the night several people entered Solomon's room and said he must go see a doctor. Staggering through the streets as if in a dream, he was led to a building, where he passed out.

He awoke to find himself sitting on a bench, handcuffed and with chains holding his ankles to a ring in the floor. With great effort, he reached his fingertips into his pocket. All his money and his free papers were gone. For several hours he sat there thinking that this was a mistake and his friends would rescue him. Then a key rattled in the lock, and two rough-looking strangers entered the dungeonlike room.

"Well, my boy, how do you feel now?" asked one of the men, a Washington, D.C., slave dealer named James Birch. Solomon replied that he was sick and demanded to know why he was in chains. Birch said that he had purchased Solomon as a slave and was about to send him down to New Orleans, Louisiana, to be sold.

"I am a free man, a resident of Saratoga Springs, where I have a wife and children who are also free, and my name is Northup!" he declared, adding that he would sue Birch upon his liberation.

Birch became furious. "You black liar, you are a runaway slave from Georgia!" he shouted. Perhaps he believed this and was just repeating a lie Brown and Hamilton had told when they sold Solomon to him. More likely, he knew the truth and was trying to crush Solomon's spirit so that he would remain quiet about his past.

Birch ordered his assistant to fetch his whip and paddle. The two men stripped Solomon of his clothing. While the assistant stood on Solomon's chains to pin him to the floor, Birch paddled him savagely. Only when his arm was exhausted did Birch pause to ask whether Solomon still claimed to be free. Solomon refused to yield, so the beating continued until the paddle broke. Years later, Solomon recalled:

*All his brutal blows could not force from my lips the foul lie that I was a slave. He [then] seized the [whip]. This was far more painful. I thought I must die beneath the lashes of the accursed brute. Even now the flesh crawls upon my bones, as I recall the scene. I was all on fire. My sufferings I can compare to nothing else than the burning agonies of hell!*

At length, Solomon no longer replied to Birch, for he was barely conscious. "If you ever again say you are entitled to your freedom, or that you have been kidnapped, you will get far worse," James Birch warned him. The two men then departed, closing the heavy iron door and leaving Solomon in darkness.

Solomon was such a trusting soul that despite his suffering he still wasn't convinced that Brown and Hamilton had sold him into slavery. They would find him and take him from this terrible place, he hoped. If not, his family would discover his whereabouts and rescue him.

Over the next few days, his hopes began to fade. He learned that he was in a slave pen so near the U.S. Capitol that he could see the building's dome when he was allowed to exercise in the yard with Birch's other slaves. Locked in his cell most of the day, with only water to drink and a little bread and fried pork to eat, he became "heartsick and discouraged," he later wrote. "Thoughts of my family, of my wife and children, continually occupied my mind. When sleep overpowered me, I dreamed of them—dreamed I was again in Saratoga, that I could see their faces, and hear their voices calling me. Awakening from the pleasant phantasms of sleep to the bitter realities around me, I could but groan and weep."

Solomon never again mentioned that he was a free man to Birch, for he knew that to do so might cost him his life. As the days passed, however, his thoughts turned to escape. The slave pen wasn't the

*The Birch slave pen, where Solomon Northup was imprisoned, in Washington, D.C.*

place from which to attempt it, though, for the building was like a fortress.

Solomon had been in the slave pen for two weeks when Birch and his assistant entered the cells with lanterns in the dead of night and woke the inmates. Solomon Northup and four other slaves, including an older man named Clem Ray, were handcuffed together and marched outside. Walking through Washington, Solomon thought of crying out for help, but the streets were deserted, and in a city where buying and selling slaves was legal who would pay attention to a black man's claim that he had been kidnapped? He considered running away, but how far could he get, handcuffed to Clem?

They walked to the Potomac River, where they were packed into the hold of a steamer among boxes of freight. A two-day trip by steamer, stagecoach, and train brought them to Richmond, Virginia, where Birch sold them to a man named Goodin and then returned to Washington, D.C., to obtain more slaves and repeat the process. Solomon spent one night in Goodin's slave pen. The next afternoon he and about forty of Goodin's other slaves were herded aboard the brig *Orleans*. After sailing down the James River into Chesapeake Bay, the ship entered the open waters of the Atlantic Ocean. Solomon had studied geography and had a better idea of where they were going than did his fellow captives. They were sailing down the Atlantic coast, probably intending to head west around Florida to New Orleans.

The brig had a crew of only six, plus the captain. During the voyage, the captives' handcuffs were removed so that they could help with the work. Solomon was placed in charge of cooking, while other slaves waited on the crew and cleaned the vessel. Off Florida, the *Orleans* encountered a violent storm and took shelter in the

*Slaves being led through Washington, D.C., in chains;
the nation's capital allowed slavery until 1862.*

Bahamas. As they awaited a favorable wind, Solomon formed a desperate plan.

He had befriended two fellow captives whose experiences had been similar to his own. Robert had been born free and had a wife and children in Cincinnati, Ohio. Two men had promised him a job in Virginia, but, once there, Robert had been kidnapped and sold to Goodin's slave pen. Arthur, a bricklayer, had long lived as a free man in Norfolk, Virginia. While passing through a white neighborhood late one night, he had been attacked by a gang and sold into slavery.

Solomon told Robert and Arthur about his plan, but before putting it into action, the three men wanted assurance that it could work.

The sailors did not count the slaves when they locked them in the ship's hold with the cargo each night. Instead of accompanying the other captives into the hold, one night Solomon hid under a small boat that lay upside down on the ship's deck. He remained beneath the boat all night. In the morning, he slipped out and joined the other slaves. None of the sailors noticed, so it appeared that the plan could succeed.

On a specified night, Solomon would hide beneath the little boat. While everyone else slept, he would climb out and release Robert and Arthur from the hold. The three of them would enter the cabin where the captain and mate slept. Robert was the captain's servant and had noticed two pistols and a cutlass in the cabin. Solomon, Robert, and Arthur would grab the weapons and take the captain and crew prisoner, shooting anyone who resisted. They would then sail the ship north to New York City, where they would tell authorities how they had been illegally seized and sold as slaves. The three men kept their plan secret, for they would undoubtedly be executed if the plot were discovered.

When a favorable wind arose, the *Orleans* left the Bahamas. And then disaster struck: Robert became ill with smallpox and soon died. He was buried at sea, about a thousand miles from his family in Cincinnati. With him died the possibility of seizing the ship, for Solomon and Arthur could not do it alone.

The vessel arrived in New Orleans four days after Robert's death. Once the ship docked, two men came aboard and informed the captain that Arthur was really free and that his kidnappers were in the Norfolk prison. Released from bondage, Arthur was "almost crazy

with delight," Solomon later recalled. "But in all the crowd that
thronged the wharf, there was no one who knew or cared for me.
There was a feeling of utter desolation in my heart, filling it with
despair and regret that I had not gone down with Robert to the bottom of the sea."

Soon the New Orleans slave trader Theophilus Freeman came on
board to take several of the captives to his slave pen. Reading from
his list, he called the slaves one by one and handcuffed them. But
when he called "Platt!" no one answered. Pointing to Solomon
Northup, he asked the captain, "Who shipped *that* nigger?"

"Birch," said the captain.

"Your name is Platt—you answer my description. Why don't you
come forward?" Freeman angrily demanded.

Solomon answered that he had never been called Platt before.

"Well, I will learn you your name!" said Freeman, cursing
Solomon and threatening to whip him if he ever again forgot that his
name was Platt. Over the next twelve years, Solomon Northup told
only one person his real name.

Solomon followed Freeman to the same Negro pen where Fed,
subsequently known as John Brown, would be bought by Jepsey
James a few years later. As was his custom, Freeman ordered
Solomon and the other newcomers to look "spry and smart" so as to
fetch a high price. Soon after his arrival, however, Solomon came
down with smallpox and had to be hospitalized. He nearly died, but
recovered after two and a half weeks and was sent back to the slave
pen. Freeman had expected to sell Solomon for $1,500, but his ill-
ness had weakened him and reduced his value. He was purchased for
$900 by a planter from central Louisiana's Red River Valley, a region
known for growing cotton and sugarcane. Solomon had now been sold

four times—each time at a profit—by Brown and Hamilton, Birch, Goodin, and now Freeman.

Solomon Northup was taken to one of the hardest places in the country for slaves to survive. It was said that gray-haired slaves were rare in this part of Louisiana, because so few of them lived to old age. Disease and overwork took a heavy death toll. Escape was nearly impossible, for the nearby swamps were crawling with snakes and alligators, and the nearest free state was five hundred miles away.

Solomon had three owners in succession—Ford, Tibaut, and Epps. Instead of Solomon Northup, he was known as Platt Ford, Platt Tibaut, and Platt Epps. Solomon grew cotton and sugarcane, did construction work, and, since the written description accompanying him said that he played the violin, he was provided with a fiddle and ordered to play jolly tunes at neighborhood dances. At night in his cabin, he often awoke yearning for home. Then he would pick up his violin and play a sad melody, its melancholy notes blending with the chorus of sounds from the nearby swamps.

Every single day, he thought about escape. He made a thousand plans and abandoned them all when he realized they were hopeless. Only once did he flee—but he did it to save his life and went just a short way.

His first owner, William Ford, was in debt to a carpenter named John Tibaut. Ford paid Tibaut by giving him Solomon, but since Solomon was worth more than the debt, Ford retained about 40 percent ownership of him.

Tibaut put Solomon to work building a corn mill and other structures. No matter how hard Solomon worked, Tibaut found fault with him, cursing and threatening him continually. An ignorant man,

Tibaut resented Solomon's intelligence and large vocabulary. Furthermore, Solomon had a proud manner, as though he didn't think of himself as a slave.

One morning, Solomon was hammering siding on a building when Tibaut accused him of using the wrong-sized nails. "God damn you, I thought you *knowed* something!" said Tibaut.

"I tried to do as you told me, master," Solomon protested, but Tibaut found a whip and ordered Solomon to remove his shirt. The rage that had built up inside him since his kidnapping suddenly burst out of Solomon, who answered, "I will *not!*" As Tibaut raised the whip, Solomon snatched it from him and threw him to the ground. In a wild fury, Solomon whipped his master and then kicked him so hard that he rolled over.

Tibaut arose slowly and stared at Solomon with murder in his eyes before riding away on his horse. For beating his master, Solomon could be put to death, so his first impulse was to run away. However, Anderson Chafin, a white man employed by Solomon's part-owner William Ford, came upon the scene and asked Solomon what had happened. Chafin sympathized with Solomon and said he knew that Tibaut was a "rascal." He warned Solomon not to run away and promised to protect him if Tibaut came back to cause more trouble.

An hour later, Tibaut returned with two other men on horseback. They dismounted and placed a rope around Solomon's neck. "Now, then," said one of Tibaut's companions, "where shall we hang the nigger?"

As they dragged him to a tree, Solomon began to cry, which amused Tibaut and his friends. Just as Solomon was about to be hanged, Chafin appeared with a pistol in each hand. "Whoever

*Solomon's last-minute rescue from hanging*

moves that slave another foot is a dead man," Chafin warned. "Platt does not deserve this treatment. You, Tibaut, are a scoundrel, and you richly deserved the flogging you received. My duty is to protect William Ford's property. Begone!" he ordered the three men. "If you have any regard for your own safety, I say, *begone!*"

Although the three men rode away, Solomon knew that Tibaut wasn't finished with him.

The story of Solomon's whipping of Tibaut spread quickly among the Red River planters. Only the fact that William Ford owned part of him saved Solomon's life. Tibaut, who owned the other 60 percent, wanted to kill Solomon, but Ford insisted that Tibaut had been at fault and that Solomon be spared. They finally agreed that Solomon should work for a few weeks on the plantation belonging to Ford's brother-in-law.

At the end of a month, Tibaut assured Ford that he was over his anger. Solomon was returned to do carpentry for Tibaut, but he remained wary, expecting Tibaut to take revenge on him at any moment. For the first two days, Chafin remained close by to protect Solomon. Thinking that the quarrel was over, on the third morning Chafin departed, leaving Tibaut and Solomon alone to build some cotton-processing machinery.

Once Chafin was gone, Tibaut criticized Solomon's work. When Solomon protested, Tibaut cried, "You're a damned liar!" Suddenly, Tibaut seized a hatchet from the workbench and sprang at Solomon. As Tibaut raised the weapon, Solomon grabbed his arm, wrestled the hatchet away, and threw it into the woods.

Next Tibaut ran with a long pole at Solomon, who knocked him to the ground and threw the weapon away. Berserk with anger, Tibaut tried to grab a large ax, but Solomon seized him by the throat and began to choke him. He was about to squeeze the life out of Tibaut when he realized, as he later wrote, that "if I killed him, my life must pay." Solomon released his grip and ran off.

He entered the Great Crocodile Swamp—vast central Louisiana wetlands that were filled with alligators, which in the 1800s were often called crocodiles. As Solomon plunged through the water, the alligators moved out of his way, but he had trouble evading the water moccasins that slithered among the fallen trees and logs. In his flight Solomon lost a shoe, and several times he nearly stepped on one of the highly poisonous snakes with his bare foot.

Tibaut fetched two friends and a pack of dogs to chase the fugitive. Solomon heard the barking coming closer as his pursuers gained on him. The dogs were within a hundred feet of him when he leaped into deeper water. Fugitives rarely escaped through the swamp, for slaves were not taught to swim and deep water afforded the best chance of a getaway. Solomon, though, had learned to swim in New York State. He swam and waded through the water until the dogs lost his scent. Wet and exhausted, he continued on through swamp and forest by moonlight. At dawn, he emerged from the woods at a farm where a young white man and his slave were catching wild hogs.

Too weary to run anymore, Solomon tried to discourage the white man from demanding to see his pass. "Where does William Ford live?" Solomon gruffly asked, trying to look fierce. Facing what appeared to be a swamp creature with tattered clothing and skin covered with bloody scratches and green swamp slime, the terrified young man pointed and said, "Seven miles from here."

About two hours later, Solomon reached Ford's plantation and told him what had happened. Ford allowed Solomon to rest a few days and then took him to Tibaut. Solomon's two owners began arguing. Ford was angry that Tibaut had tried to kill Solomon, while Tibaut treated the episode as if it had been a foxhunt. "I never saw such running before," said Tibaut. "I'll bet a hundred dollars, he'll beat any nigger in Louisiana. I offered [a friend] twenty-five dollars to catch him, dead or alive, but he outran his dogs in a fair race. Somehow he got the dogs off the track, and we had to give up the hunt. The boys said he was drowned, sure. Oh, he's a cuss to run, this nigger is!"

During that time, they should not talk much together, or Epps might become suspicious.

By autumn, the Epps house was finished and still nothing had come of the letters. Solomon feared that the recipients had died or moved away, or that the Marksville postmaster had become suspicious and had destroyed the letters. The night before his departure from the new Epps house, Bass briefly spoke to Solomon in private. He said that he would return to visit the Epps family for a day or two at Christmastime. If nothing had happened by then, he assured Solomon, he would take further action.

True to his word, Bass rode to the Epps plantation on Christmas Eve. Early Christmas morning, he slipped out of the house that he and Solomon had helped build and visited Solomon in his cabin. "There is a better way to manage this business than writing letters," Bass told him. "I have a job or two which can be completed by March or April. By that time I shall have a considerable sum of money, and then, Platt, I am going to Saratoga Springs myself. If I can get you away from here, it will be a good act that I shall like to think of all of my life. And I shall succeed, Platt. Don't be discouraged. I'm with you, life or death." Samuel Bass then left Solomon's cabin and returned to the guest room in the Epps house.

Solomon didn't have to wait until March or April. One of Samuel Bass's letters had been forwarded to Solomon's family, who had moved from Saratoga Springs to nearby Glens Falls. The letter was the best possible news for Anne and the children, for it revealed that Solomon was alive and in bondage near Marksville, Louisianna. Anne wrote to New York's governor, Washington Hunt, who became involved in the case. Governor Hunt appointed the lawyer Henry B. Northup, a relative of the man who had owned Solomon's father, to visit Marksville with papers stating that Solomon Northup was a free man and must be released immediately.

As Solomon Northup and Samuel Bass spoke in Solomon's cabin on Christmas morning of 1852, Henry B. Northup was on his way to Louisiana. He arrived in Marksville on January 1, 1853, and showed his letters and documents to local authorities. There was still a giant obstacle to locating Solomon, however. To protect him in case the letter fell into the wrong hands, Bass had not explained that Solomon was now called Platt or that he lived on the Epps plantation.

Henry B. Northup couldn't find anyone in Marksville who recognized the name "Solomon Northup," so he decided to undertake a monumental task: He would go from plantation to plantation around Marksville, describing Solomon and asking if anyone knew him. This plan probably would have failed, for there were thousands of slaves in the vicinity and the Epps plantation was eighteen miles from town. Fortunately, while discussing slavery with a lawyer in Marksville, Henry B. Northup inquired whether there were any abolitionists in town. "One," answered the lawyer. "An eccentric creature who preaches abolitionism vehemently. He is a generous man, but always maintains the wrong side of an argument. He is a carpenter. His name is Bass."

Henry B. Northup visited Bass and explained his mission. "I saw him Christmas, a week ago today," said Bass, hoping that Northup had really come to rescue Solomon. "He is the slave of Edwin Epps. He is not known as Solomon Northup. He is called Platt."

On Monday, January 3, 1853, Solomon and several other slaves were picking cotton—slowly, because their fingers were numb from the cold. Saying he had a way to warm them, Epps went to his house to get his whip. While he was gone, a carriage arrived at the plantation and two men stepped out. As they approached through the cot-

*Solomon reunited with his family (this and the earlier three drawings showing Solomon are illustrations from his book,* Twelve Years a Slave*)*

"They embraced me," Solomon wrote, "and with tears flowing down their cheeks, hung upon my neck. When our emotions had subsided we gathered round the fire, and conversed of the thousand events that had occurred—the hopes and fears, the joys and sorrows, the trials and troubles we had each experienced during the long separation." Solomon was told that his mother had died but his son, Alonzo, was healthy and away on a visit to western New York. Margaret was married and had a son, who had been named Solomon Northup Staunton for the grandfather he had never seen.

The two men who had kidnapped Solomon were arrested, as was James Birch, proprietor of the slave pen in Washington, D.C. But the three men lied in court, and were dismissed on account of legal technicalities and lack of evidence. Apparently, Epps never discovered that Samuel Bass had written the letters that freed Solomon Northup. Bass remained in Marksville, where he died of pneumonia eight months after securing Solomon's freedom.

Solomon and Anne Northup and their family lived in Glens Falls for the next several years. Solomon wrote a book titled *Twelve Years a Slave,* which for a time was very popular, but he soon dropped from view and quietly worked as a carpenter for the rest of his life. It appears that Solomon Northup died in his early fifties, around the time that the Civil War broke out in 1861.

# CHAPTER TWELVE

# HARRIET TUBMAN

## *"My People Are Free!"*

*Except for the determined look in her eyes, the woman called Moses wasn't physically impressive. Only five feet tall, she was missing her upper front teeth and had a big dent in her head. Many people who met her at first thought she was half-witted, for the head injury she suffered as a teenager made her fall asleep three or four times a day, often in the midst of a task. Yet this little woman was the most daring and successful of all Underground Railroad conductors. After escaping bondage, she made many trips back into the slave states, leading more than three hundred men, women, and children north to freedom. Southern slave owners became so exasperated at her ability to evade capture that they offered $40,000 for her head. She was a legendary figure even in her own lifetime, and her name was Harriet Tubman.*

Harriet was born in Bucktown, a village on Maryland's Eastern Shore near Chesapeake Bay, in about 1820. Her parents, a slave couple named Harriet (known as Rit) and Benjamin, had eleven children, several of whom were sold into slavery in the Deep South. From the time she was six years old, Harriet was hired out to neighbors by her owner, a planter named Edward Brodas. She worked for a weaver. She tended a man's muskrat traps, wading through cold water so often that she became very ill and had to be sent home. She served as a house slave.

At the age of nine, Harriet went to work as a housekeeper and baby-sitter for a Miss Susan, who whipped her five or six times a day. After her day's chores, Harriet spent the night in Miss Susan's room, caring for Miss Susan's baby. Sometimes while rocking the cradle Harriet dozed off, and the baby's cries awakened its mother. Then Miss Susan would grab the whip from the shelf and lash Harriet across her head. Eighty years later, Harriet's neck still bore scars from Miss Susan's whip. Miss Susan barely fed Harriet and eventually sent the half-starved girl back to her owner with the comment that she was worthless.

Mr. Brodas began to suspect that Harriet was defiant and wasn't trying to please her employers. He was right. From childhood, Harriet hadn't been able to understand why white people controlled everything, while her parents couldn't even keep their own children.

Upon entering her teens, Harriet was hired out as a field hand. One autumn night, a fellow slave left the plantation where Harriet was working and went to a store without asking permission. The overseer followed the man into the store, intending to whip him as a reminder that slaves couldn't come and go as they pleased. Harriet trailed the two men, apparently to beg the overseer to show mercy to the slave. The overseer ignored her pleas, however, and ordered her to help him seize the man.

She refused, blocking the doorway to prevent the overseer from pursuing the slave as he ran off. Suddenly, the overseer picked up a

*Harriet Tubman*

jar or other heavy object from the store counter and threw it toward the fleeing man, missing him but striking Harriet a terrific blow on the head and nearly killing her. It took her months to recover, and she was left with a large dent in her skull. Thereafter, she suffered "spells of sleep" every few hours. Awakening from these short blackouts, she would resume what she had been doing, not even realizing that she had been unconscious.

After her injury, Harriet became extremely religious. She prayed that Mr. Brodas would stop selling members of her family and his other slaves. "O Lord," she prayed, "convert Master, change that man's heart!" But he continued in his ways, and probably would have sold Harriet farther south to a cotton or rice plantation had her injury not made her damaged goods. She then prayed, "O Lord, if you aren't ever going to change that man's heart, kill him, Lord, and take him out of the way!" About a year later Brodas died and Harriet's family went to a new master, Anthony Thompson, a preacher around Bucktown.

Harriet's father, Ben, was a lumberjack. A lumberman named John Stewart hired him and Harriet from Reverend Thompson. Ben supervised a crew that cut down timber for the Baltimore shipyards. When she wasn't otherwise occupied on Stewart's plantation, Harriet helped her father. Happy to be working near him, she made up songs as she chopped wood, drove oxen, and plowed. Harriet grew so strong that Mr. Stewart invited his friends over just to watch her pick up barrels of flour or lift tree trunks.

In her mid-twenties, Harriet married John Tubman, a free black man, and moved into his cabin. Although she loved John, he gave her little besides his last name. When she proposed that they flee to the North so that she could also be free, he made fun of the idea.

She made her first escape attempt in 1849, at the age of twenty-nine. After a rumor spread that Reverend Thompson was about to sell his slaves to the Deep South, Harriet persuaded three of her brothers to run away with her. They didn't get far. The brothers soon became frightened and returned to Reverend Thompson's plantation, insisting that Harriet go back with them.

Within days of her return, Harriet learned that Reverend Thompson really *was* determined to sell her, no matter how low the price, so she decided to set out alone. Later, she described her thoughts at this time: "There's two things I've got a right to and these are death or liberty. One or the other I mean to have. No one will take me back alive! I shall fight for my liberty!"

Harriet wanted to say good-bye to her family, but if she told them she was leaving, they might be punished as her accomplices. She decided to hint at her plans by singing as she walked past their cabins:

> I'm sorry, friends, to leave you,
> Farewell! oh, farewell!
> But I'll meet you in the morning,
> Farewell! oh, farewell!
>
> I'll meet you in the morning,
> Safe in the Promised Land,
> On the other side of Jordan,
> Bound for the Promised Land.

Harriet often sang spirituals—religious folk songs—so nobody thought much about this one until the next day, when she was missing. Then everyone who had heard her realized that her song had had a double meaning. The Promised Land was the biblical land of Israel, to which Moses led the Jewish people, but Harriet also intended it to mean the northern United States, where she hoped to be free.

Traveling by night, with the North Star as her guide, Harriet headed toward the Promised Land. Several people helped her, including a white woman for whom she had made a bed quilt and a farmer who hid her in his wagon and drove her a short way. After traveling more than a hundred miles, mostly on foot, in several weeks she reached Pennsylvania. On the day in 1849 that she first reached free soil, the entire world suddenly appeared different. "I looked at my hands to see if I was the same person," she later told a friend. "There was such a glory over everything. The Sun came like gold through the trees, and over the fields, and I felt like I was in Heaven."

She went to Philadelphia, where she found work cooking, cleaning, and washing clothes. From Philadelphia she moved to Cape May, New Jersey, where she worked at similar jobs. Although it was a wonderful new feeling to earn money and go where she wanted, Harriet made a sad discovery. She couldn't truly enjoy her freedom while her parents, her brothers and sisters, and so many others remained in bondage. She made a plan that was common among fugitive slaves but that was rarely carried out: She would return to the South and lead her loved ones to freedom.

Difficult before, rescuing slaves from the South became nearly impossible with the adoption of the 1850 Fugitive Slave Law. Even fugitives in such seemingly safe places as Boston now fled farther north, to Canada. Virtually no runaway slave headed back south— except Harriet Tubman.

Harriet did some investigating, learning the names and locations of people along the UGRR. She began with her sister Mary Ann and her family. Since Harriet couldn't read or write, she had a friend write to Mary Ann instructing her what to do. In December 1850, Mary Ann and her two children escaped from Reverend Thompson and traveled by boat to Baltimore, Maryland. Meanwhile, Harriet slipped into Baltimore. She met her relatives at a secret location, where they all hid for a while. Then, probably with the help of friends, Harriet led Mary Ann and her children out of the closely patrolled city. She took the fugitives north to freedom, stopping at UGRR stations along the way.

Encouraged by this success, Harriet returned to the Thompson plantation a few months later and helped one of her brothers run away, along with two other men. Also in 1851, she led a party of eleven people to St. Catharines, Canada, north of Buffalo, New York. By then, slave hunters were constantly on the watch for her, so she decided it was too dangerous for her to live in the United States. From 1851 to 1857, she lived in St. Catharines—when she wasn't off helping slaves escape.

Harriet gradually expanded her field of operations beyond Maryland, including states in the Deep South. In all, she made about twenty trips to rescue slaves. She later related some of her experiences to a few friends, so we know a little about her many hairbreadth escapes.

The trips *into* slave territory were relatively easy, because slave hunters didn't expect a fugitive to head south. To conceal the dent in her skull that would have given away her identity, she wore a colorful bandanna. She also devised a trick of making herself appear elderly, walking hunched over, as though bent with age. Generally she needed no disguise, however, for who would suspect that the small, ordinary-looking woman was the famous Harriet Tubman?

She instructed friends to use a secret code when they informed slaves that she was coming. For example, she sent her brothers this message: "Tell my brothers to be always watching unto prayer, and when the good old ship of Zion comes along, to be ready to step aboard." Of course, she was really telling them to be ready to escape with her.

As she made rescue after rescue, the slaves began to call her

Moses, after the biblical hero who led the Jewish people out of slav-ery in Egypt and to the Promised Land. At her approach, slaves would whisper, "Moses is coming to take us away"—away from the South, which Harriet called the Land of Egypt.

She usually set out with a group of slaves on a Saturday night, when planters attended parties and dances and didn't guard their property as closely as usual. Often she not only led off a master's slaves but also stole his horse and buggy, the better to transport them. She hid the slaves beneath piles of straw or vegetables in the buggy. White people who saw her on the road assumed she was a free black woman, for what fugitive slave would dare drive a buggy in the open? Harriet's many escapes by buggy earned her another nickname: Old Chariot. After driving all night Saturday and all day Sunday, when the roads were clear because people were in church, she would aban-don the vehicle and continue with the group on foot, traveling after sunset.

She took the runaways through swamps, forests, and other thinly populated areas. If there were babies with no parents, Harriet carried them in a basket on her arm. Sometimes, a runaway became fearful and wanted to return and surrender, which would endanger the rest of the group if he were forced to reveal their whereabouts. Then Harriet would pull out the loaded revolver she kept in her pocket and threaten, "You go on or die!" Later the fainthearted fugitive would thank her for making him continue on to freedom.

Harriet was said to have a sixth sense. Whenever she suspected trouble, she hid her passengers in the nearest safe place. Reportedly, she once hid a group in a pile of manure with straws in their mouths so they could breathe. Often she walked apart from the main group to scout ahead. Talking aloud was risky, so she communicated with her passengers by singing. The famous spiritual "Go Down, Moses" became known as her fighting song. If she sang a few words of it twice, the group knew the coast was clear. But if she sang it only once, they knew to hide because someone was coming. The person approaching would see only a lone black woman, apparently singing to herself.

Tubman and her passengers stopped at many UGRR stations en route to the northern states or Canada. Recognizing her secret rap on their doors, stationmasters hid Harriet and her followers in barns, chimneys, attics, and "potato holes" dug by farmers for storing crops.

Thomas Garrett's home in Wilmington, Delaware, was a favorite stop of Harriet's. This Quaker abolitionist sheltered and aided about 2,500 escaped slaves in his lifetime. Once when the Wilmington bridge was heavily guarded by police looking for Harriet, she and Garrett planned a daring move. Garrett arranged to send two wagon-loads of bricklayers across the bridge as if they were going to work. The guards allowed them to pass and assumed that they would cross back over the bridge at the end of the day. Later the bricklayers *did* recross the bridge—only this time Harriet and her passengers were hiding in the wagons, beneath the bricks.

Occasionally, Harriet traveled with her passengers by train. Several times when she thought she had been recognized she temporarily switched to a southbound train. The railroad conductors concluded that the little woman couldn't possibly be escaping with slaves, for why would they be heading south?

Friends began to beg Harriet to end her UGRR activities, for rewards totaling $40,000 (equal to approximately $800,000 in today's money) were being offered for her capture, dead or alive. It was said that slaveholders preferred to capture her alive so they

*Illustration from William Still's book,* The Underground Railroad; *the bent-over woman near the middle is believed to be Harriet Tubman.*

could burn her to death. She seemed unconcerned about the danger, saying, "If the time comes for me to go, the Lord will take me."

In 1857, Harriet Tubman settled in the town of Auburn, in central New York State. That year she learned that her father had been caught helping a slave escape and was about to be punished. Her parents were in their seventies—well beyond the age when escape seemed possible—but that didn't stop Harriet.

She returned to Reverend Thompson's plantation, visited her parents, and told them she had come to take them away. She rigged up

# AFTERWORD

## *Slavery Is Still with Us*

In 1853, Solomon Northup predicted in his book, *Twelve Years a Slave,* that the nation would suffer "a terrible day of vengeance" because of slavery. Five years later, Abraham Lincoln said, "A house divided against itself cannot stand. I believe this government cannot endure permanently, half slave and half free." The war over slavery began on April 12, 1861. Northerners called it the War of Southern Rebellion. To southerners it was the War of Northern Aggression. Today we remember it as the Civil War, or the War Between the States. Truly a "terrible day of vengeance," the Civil War claimed the lives of more than 600,000 soldiers—the most American military deaths in any war ever fought, up to the present day.

When the fighting began, there were more than four million slaves in the South. By the time the South surrendered on April 9, 1865, Union troops had freed most of them. On December 6, 1865—eight months after the conflict ended—the Thirteenth Amendment to the U.S. Constitution was adopted, and the remaining slaves were freed. With slavery ended in the United States, thousands of African Americans who had taken refuge in Canada

196

or the northern states returned to the South. Some remained in Canada, however. Many of the 600,000 black people living in Canada today are descendants of fugitive slaves who sought refuge there 150 years ago or more.

Following the Civil War, slavery was outlawed in Cuba, Brazil, and many other lands. Yet even today slavery still exists in parts of South America, Asia, and Africa. The United Nations, which works to establish world peace and to help humanity, says that slavery and slavery-like practices "remain a grave and persistent problem." The UN estimates that 100 million children around the world live in bondage. Many are slaves in the traditional sense. They work in mines and build roads and are chained up at night to prevent their escape. Millions of other children suffer under slavery-like conditions. These children, some just seven years old, work twelve to fourteen hours a day and are paid very little. Unable to attend school and poorly fed, they live much like the American slaves of long ago.

There are also millions of adult slaves. "Debt bondage" keeps many families enslaved. In some countries, a family that owes a person money must work for him until the debt is paid. Often the debt is too big ever to be repaid. Generation after generation, the debtors and their children and grandchildren must work on the rich person's farm or in his factory.

Long ago, people like Harriet Tubman, William Still, Levi and Katie Coffin, and the citizens of Oberlin, Ohio, dedicated themselves to rescuing their fellow Americans from slavery. Today it is up to a new generation to complete the struggle worldwide. To find out what you can do to combat slavery, contact the UN at either of these addresses:

Pickard, Kate. *The Kidnapped and the Ransomed.* Philadelphia: The Jewish Publication Society of America, 1970 (reprint of 1856 edition).

Prince, Mary. *The History of Mary Prince, A West Indian Slave, Related by Herself.* London: Pandora Press, 1987 (reprint of 1831 edition).

Sterling, Dorothy. *Black Foremothers: Three Lives.* New York: The Feminist Press, 2nd ed., 1988.

Still, William. *The Underground Railroad.* New York: Arno Press and The New York Times, 1968 (reprint of 1872 edition).

*Two Biographies by African-American Women* (includes reprint of 1856 edition of *Biography of an American Bondman* by Josephine Brown). New York: Oxford University Press, 1991.

Winks, Robin W. *The Blacks in Canada: A History.* New Haven, Conn.: Yale University Press, 1971.

## *WEB SITES*

You can find more information about fugitive slaves on the Internet by searching for "Underground Railroad." Some particularly good sites are listed below.

The National Geographic site lets you imagine what it would be like to be a fugitive slave. This site has excellent links and can be found at:
www.nationalgeographic.com/features/99/railroad

Information about the Levi Coffin House in Indiana can be found at:
www.waynet.org/nonprofit.coffin.htm

The Oberlin College (Ohio) site is also helpful. The address is:
www.oberlin.edu/~EOG/OYTT/ch7.html

# PICTURE CREDITS

# INDEX

Page numbers in **bold** type refer to illustrations.

abolitionists:
    arguments of, xv, 40, 41, 174
    in Oberlin, Ohio, 111–29, **124, 126**
    secret words of, 35
    slaves' freedom purchased by, 148
Adams, William, 76, 77, 79
American and Foreign Anti-Slavery
    Society, 153
Anderson, John, 130–46, 131
    arrest and trial of, 140–45
    autobiography of, 145–46
    birth and family of, 130–31
    in Canada, 137–45, 153
    in England, 145–46
    escape of, 134–36
Ashburton, Lord, 141

Bacon, John, 114, 115, 121
Bass, Samuel, 174–78, 181
bells and horns, 21–22, **22**
*Beloved* (Morrison), 43
Benford, *see* Fed
Bigelow, J., 148, 149, 151
*Biography of an American Bondman*
    (Brown), 110
Birch, James, 160–64, 166, 167, 181
Boynton, Shakespeare, 116–18
Bradford, Sarah, 195
British Empire, 1, 9, 11; *see also*
    England
Brodas, Edward, 183, 185
Brown, Henry "Box," 66–75, **71, 75,** 77
Brown, John (Fed), 28–31
Brown, Josephine, 110
Brown, Merrill, 158–61, 167
Brown, William Wells, 94, 97–110, **98**
    books written by, 109–10

Brown, William Wells (*cont.*)
    journey to freedom of, 105–8
    name of, 107–8
Buchanan, James, 113, 125, 141
Burton, Mr. and Mrs. Moses, 130–33

Canada:
    Anderson's arrest and trial in, 140–45
    black communities in, 130, 137, 139
    England and, 140–44
    as fugitives' goal, 105–6, 108, 114,
        134–35, 136, 149, 153, 187
    fugitives in, 30, 36, 37, 95, 124,
        137–40, **138,** 197–98
    slave hunters in, 130, 137, 139
    slavery illegal in, 40, 112, 134, 142
Chafin, Anderson, 168–70
Chase, Salmon Portland, 126
children in present-day bondage, 198
Cincinnati, Ohio, 37–38, 41, 60
Civil War, xvi, 37, 96, 144, 146, 193,
    **194,** 197
*Clotel* (Brown), 109–10
Coffin, Katie, 29, 35–38, **36,** 40
Coffin, Levi, xvi, 29, 35–38, **36,** 40,
    42–43
Collins, Robert and Eliza, 84–85
Concklin, Seth, 61–63
Cook, Grove, 99
cotton industry, xiii, **16,** 25–26, **26**
Craft, Ellen, 80–96, **82**
    birth father of, 81–83
    book by, 96
    disguise of, **83,** 86–88, 150
    in England, 95–96
    escape of, 88–93, 108
    husband of, *see* Craft, William

Craft, William, 80–81, **84,** 85–96
   birth and family of, 85–86
   book by, 96
   in England, 95–96
   escape of, 88–93, 108
   wife of, *see* Craft, Ellen

Davis, James, 14–15
Davis, Nelson, 195
debt bondage, 198
Declaration of Independence, xi, xiii, 174
Digges, Ben, 135, 136
Digges, Seneca, 135–36, 140, 142, 145
Doctor H., 150–52

England:
   Anderson in, 145–46
   Canada and, 140–44
   Crafts in, 95–96
   Fed in, 30–31
   Mary Prince in, 8–11
   Parliament of, 11
   slavery ended in, **10,** 11, 18, 95,
      113
Epps, Edwin, 172–81
*Escape, The* (Brown), 110

Fairchild, James and Mary, 123–24
families, **53**
   separation of, xiv, 2–3, **3,** 77, 84,
      85–86, 99, 131
   of slave mothers, 41–43, **42,** 50, 82,
      100–101, 133
   slaves' inability to protect, xiv, 52,
      69–70, 84, 99
Fed, 12–31, **13**
   autobiography of, 31
   in England, 30–31
   escape attempts of, 18–20, 22–24,
      26–31
   as John Brown, 28–31
   punishment of, 16–17, 18, 20–22

Fed (*cont.*)
   sale of, 15, 16, 24–25, 166
   sawmill invention of, 30
field slaves, xiii, xiv, 84, 172
Fillmore, Millard, 39, 94
Ford, William, 167, 168, 169–72
Frank (fugitive), 114–18
free blacks, kidnap of, 155–56, 158–62,
      165, 173, 181
freedom, 155
   friends' purchase of, 109, 148
   instinct for, 43, 77, 140, 186
   slaves' purchase of their own, 7–8, 44,
      48, 53–57, 64, 132
Freeman, Rev. A. N., 153–54
Freeman, Theophilus, 24–25, 166–67
Friedman, Isaac, 53–58, 60, 61
Friedman, Joseph, 53–56
fugitives, **21, 103, 113, 117, 194**
   extradition of, 141–44
   North Star as guide for, xv, 29, 102,
      **106, 127,** 186
   punishment for helping, 39–40, 63,
      74, 191
   punishment of, xv, 86, 104
   rewards for return of, **28,** 135, **143,**
      149, 153
Fugitive Slave Law, **93,** 149
   adoption of, 39–40, 112, 187
   Crafts and, 94–95
   Fed and, 27
   free blacks and, 156
   Henry "Box" Brown and, 74
   Higher Law vs., 40, 113, 125, 128
   John Price and, 120, 121
   Margaret Garner and, 41–42
   Oberlin trial and, 125–26, 128
   Still family and, 62–63
   William Brown and, 108–9

Garner, Margaret, 38–43, **42,** 114
Garner, Robert, 38, 41, 43

Garrett, Thomas, 190
Gillet, Matthew, 125
Gist, Levi, 50, 52
Gist, Nat, 47–48, 49, 50
Glasgow, John, 17–18, 22, 30
Goodin's slave pen, 163, 164–65, 167
Green, Lear, 76–79, **78**
Griffin, Peter, *see* Still, Peter
Griffin, Saunders, 44–45
Grimes, Harry, 66

Hamilton, Abram, 158–61, 167
Harris, Eliza, 32–37, 153
Harrison, William Henry, 159
Haviland, Laura, 36, 137–39
Hayden, Harriet and Lewis, 94
*History of Mary Prince, The* (Prince), 10–11
Hogun, John Henry, 55
house slaves, xiii, 84, 85, 98
Hunt, Washington, 176
Hurd, Buck, 18–19

Illinois, as free state, 27, 136

James, Daniel, 7–8
James, Jepsey, 25–28, 166
Jennings, Anderson, 116, 118, 119–22, 126, 128

*Kidnapped and the Ransomed, The* (Still), 64
Kite, Elijah, 38, 41

Lake Erie, 108, 114, 116
Langston, Charles, 125, 128
Langston, John Mercer, 111, 125
Lee, Elizabeth, 99, 100, 104–5, 110
    escape attempt of, 101–3
    rape of, 97–98
Lee, Simon, 97
Lincoln, Abraham, 37, 144, 197
Lincoln, William, 121–22, 125–26

Louisiana:
    Great Crocodile Swamp in, 170–71
    slavery in, 166–67
lying-out, 19
Lyman, Ansel, 119, 121, 125

Maria (Ellen's mother), 82, 84, 85
Massachusetts, as free state, xiii, 64–65, 74, 93, 94, 95, 111
McDaniel, Col. Reuben, 133–36
McKiernan, Bernard, 51, 52, 62–65
Montgomery, Col. James, 193
Moore, Betty, 12–14, 25
Moravian Church, 9
Morrison, Toni, 43
Mott, Lucretia, 74
Murrell, John, 18–19

names, xiv, 12, 36, 107, 156
Nancy (Fed's mother), 12–15
Nancy (Henry's wife), 68–70, 74
*Narrative of Henry Box Brown* (Brown), 74
*Narrative of William Wells Brown* (Brown), 109
neck chain and shackles, **152**
Negro speculators, 100
Negro stealers, 18–19
New Orleans, 23–25, 165–66
Noble, James, 76–77
North Star, as guide for travelers, xv, 29, 102, **106, 127,** 186
Northup, Anne Hampton, 156–57, 158, 173, 176, **180,** 180, 181
Northup, Henry B., 157, 176–79, **178**
Northup, Solomon, 155–81, **157, 169**
    autobiography of, **180,** 181, 197
    Bass and, 174–78
    Epps and, 167, 172–81
    escape attempts of, 164–65, 170–73
    freedom regained by, 178–81
    Henry and, 176–79, **178**

Northup Solomon, (*cont.*)
    kidnap and sale of, 160–63, 166–67
    as Platt, 166–70, 173, 175, 177, 178

Oberlin, Ohio:
    abolitionists in, 111–29, **124, 126**
    arrests and trial in, 125–26, 128–29,
       141
    Price's escape to, 114–16
    Price's rescue in, 119–24, 125, 128
    slave hunters in, 112, 116–19, 128
Oberlin-Wellington Rescuers, 119–29
Ohio, as free state, 38, 105, 121, 128
Ohio River, crossing the ice on, 32–33,
    **34**, 37, 38, 114–15
overseers, xiv, 5, 52, 68, 99

Packard, Kate, 64
Peck, Henry, 125
Pennsylvania Anti-Slavery Society, 58, 59,
    60, 75, 94
Philadelphia, 58–59, 93–94, 111
Plumb, Ralph, 125
Price, Charles, 147, 149
Price, Enoch, 105, 109
Price, John, 111–29
    escape to Oberlin, 114–16
    name of, 116
    Oberlin rescue of, 119–24, 125, 128
    slave hunters and, 116–21, 124, 126,
       128
Prince, Mary, 1–11
    autobiography of, 10–11
    Daniel and, 7–8
    in England, 8–11
    Parliament and, 11
Pringle, Margaret and Thomas, 9

Quakers, 28–29, 107–8, 115, 190

Rankin, Rev. John, 34–35
rape, xiv, 82, 97–98, 147

Ray, Clem, 163, 173
*Reminiscences of Levi Coffin* (Coffin), 37,
    42–43
runaways, *see* fugitives

*Scenes in the Life of Harriet Tubman*
    (Bradford), 195
Schooner, Elizabeth, 108
Scott, John, 121, 122
shackles and neck chain, **152**
Shipherd, John, 111
slave hunters:
    Ann Maria Weems and, 149, 153
    in Canada, 130, 137, 139
    Eliza Harris and, 33
    Fed and, 28
    John Anderson and, 136–39
    John Price and, 116–21, 126, 128
    law and, 39, **93**, 94–95, **117**, 156
    Margaret Garner and, 41–42, **42**
    in Oberlin, 112, 116–18, 128
    Still family and, 44, 62–64
    William Brown and, 102–3
slave life, xiv–xvi, 84
    written records of, xv–xvii, 10–11,
       31, 74, 96, 109–10, 145–46, 181
*Slave Life in Georgia* (Brown), 31
slave markets, **39**
    ads for, **xvi, 7, 67**
    auctions in, **xviii**, 2–3, **40**
    Negro pens in, 24–25, 161, **162**
    preparation for, 15, 25, 100
slavery, present-day, 197–99
slave trade, **x**, xi, xii, **xiii, xiv**, 12
Smith, Maj. James, 81–84
Smith, Samuel A., 70–72, 73, 74–75
soul drivers, 100
southern states:
    Civil War and, 144, 197
    cotton in, xiii, **16**, 25–26, **26**
    plantations in, **49, 53**
    slavery in, xiii, **134**

Staunton, Solomon Northup, 180
Stevens, Decatur, 19, 20–21, 22, 23
Stevens, Thomas, 16–18, 19
Stewart, Philo, 111
Still, Charity, 44–46, **47**, 59
Still, Levin, 44–51, 58, 59
Still, Peter, 44–65, **45**
  birth and childhood of, 44–46
  buying freedom, 53–57, 64
Still, Vina, 51–53, **57**, 61–65
Still, William, **47**
  Ann Maria Weems and, 149–52
  Crafts and, 93–94
  family of, 46, 58–59, 65
  Henry "Box" Brown and, 72–74, **75**
  Lear Green and, 79
  Peter and, 58–59, 61, 63–65
  Tubman and, 192
  Underground Railroad and, xvi, 35,
    59–60, 79
*Story of the Life of John Anderson*
    (Anderson and Twelvetrees), 146
Stowe, Harriet Beecher, 37

Tappan, Arthur, 153
Tappan, Lewis, 141, 152–53, 154
Thirteenth Amendment, 197
Thompson, Anthony, 185, 187, 191
Thompson, John, 66
Tibaut, John, 167–72
Tomlin, Lewis, 132, 135, 137, 138–39
Tomlin, Maria, 132–37, 139, 146
Tubman, Harriet, 182–95, **184**
  in Civil War, 193
  journey of, 186–87
  religion and, 184–85
  schools established by, 193
  Underground Railroad and, 35, 182,
    187–92, **191**
Tubman, John, 185, 195
Turks Islands, 4–6
Twelvetrees, Harper, 145–46

*Twelve Years a Slave* (Northup), **180,**
    181, 197

*Uncle Tom's Cabin* (Stowe), **34,** 37
"Underground Railroad" (sculpture), **126**
Underground Railroad (UGRR), xv, 149
  Coffins and, 35–38
  Eliza Harris and, 34–37
  Fed and, 29–30
  John Anderson and, 136–37
  Lear Green and, 79
  Margaret Garner and, 38, 43
  in Oberlin, 112, 122–23, **126**
  records of, xvi, 59–60
  Tubman and, 35, 182, 187–92, **191**
  William Still and, xvi, 35, 59–60,
    79
*Underground Railroad, The* (Still), 60
Underground Railroad Quilt, **127**
United Nations, 198–99
United States:
  Canada, England, and, 140–44
  Civil War in, *see* Civil War
  free vs. slave states in, xiii, **134**
  Revolution of, 97

Virginia, slave trade in, xi, **xiv, xviii,** 163

Wadsworth, Loring, 125
Wadsworth Hotel, Wellington, Ohio,
    119–22, **120**
Washington, D.C., slavery in, 159, 161,
    **162, 164**
Webster, Daniel, 141
Webster-Ashburton Treaty, 141, 142
Weems, Ann Maria, 147–54, **148**
whippings, xiv, xv, 3–4, 14, 17, 18, 21, 26,
    48–49, 133, 147, **150,** 161
Winsor, Richard, 122, 125
Wright, Joe (Weems), **148,** 150–52

Young, John, 97–99, 100, 103–4